Burn Your Fat Pants: Candid Guidance from a Girlfriend

About The Author

De'Anna Nunez is founder of the Mind Body Fit Club national weight loss program, and Contributing Editor for Active.com. De'Anna is a Certified Hypnotherapist, Certified Nutrition Specialist and NLP Practitioner. Her expertise in weight loss has helped thousands of women in their quest to uncovering their best body. A Marathon runner and exercise enthusiast, De'Anna brings an abundance of motivation to the lives of her readers and clients.

Published by SAVVYGIRLPRESS

Nunez, De'Anna 2011

Burn Your Fat Pants / Candid guidance from a girlfriend on how to ditch diets, lose weight and love yourself more by De'Anna Nunez

ISBN 978-0-9838684-0-8

Printed in the United States of America

Book Coach & Editing: Amanda Johnson
Editor: Suzanne Hodges
Layout & Design: Suzanne Hodges
Cover Photo: Nicole Caldwell
MBFC Photo Shoot: Keith Bates

Contents

Special Thanks

There were specific people that gave me direction or insight who greatly contributed to me writing this book, and they absolutely must be recognized.

To Genelle June Bucsemi, for your unconditional love and belief in me. You are an incredible friend. I am so thankful that you entered my life.

Jaylene Welch, your inspiring example to walk through the fire and come out the other side one hundred pounds lighter. Your journey has been a gift for all of us. You have the wings of an angel.

Carol Wegleitner for your adventurous spirit and ability to dissect, learn and find a solution in every situation. I see you.

To Marcia Goettege for your undeniable enthusiasm. Your zest for life is contagious!

Wendy Basulto, for your willingness to lay it on the line, push through and be a warrior. I am so appreciative to have witnessed true moments of courage.

Trish Kelley for suggesting I run a half marathon; you had no idea what you were starting.

Kim Page for believing in the HypnoThin program and providing the face of change.

Jeanette Bunn for being a seriously kick-ass chick. I admire your incredible drive and focused optimism. Diane Sharp for being a Mom that is lighthearted, youthful and wise; I am so lucky to have inherited you. I love you both as my own.

Eva and Theresa for your technical support and offering to give of yourself. It meant so much to me at crunch time. Thank you for opening the door of possibility.

To KB, for joining in on the crusade and always being down for the cause. I don't know of one other person like you. You are genuine to the core. Thanks for the many laughs. Muah!

My Mom, for unknowingly giving me a platform. You have brought me incredible lessons. I am so appreciative of your continued love and support.

To Dad & Terri, thank you for your unconditional love and support...always.

Michelle for showing me just how strong the resistance can be, and how important it is that I am relentless.

Erin Grimes for your lifelong friendship. Your honesty and kindness has softened my edges. I love you.

Amanda Johnson for your guidance and coaching through this writing and editing process. You are wonderfully gifted.

Suzanne Hodges, thanks for showing up when I asked God for you. I am so incredibly grateful for your knowledge, skill and talent. Believe in the gift.

My Grandma, for jogging thirty minutes every morning (even at age 85) with a tissue in your hand, blotting the sweat from your brow. For patting me on the knee, and the loving stories you told me over and over and over.

My husband Troy, my rock, my lover. Your patience is exemplary. I love that there is nothing you can't do. And for your rockn' abs that you so effortlessly possess. (insert sarcastic eye roll & head shake here. I am forever perplexed at how easy it is for you.) My kids: My handsome Zach, cutie pie Vasco and sweet Lil Savvy. You are my world.

Introduction

I awake to the sun shining through my sliding glass door. It's a beautiful morning. The Blue Jays are chirping and swinging on the bird feeder outside my bedroom. I feel wonderfully rested. I think, "Dang I needed that good night's sleep; I've been so stressed lately." I stretch my arms toward the ceiling and am ready to start my day.

Then, a flash of reality hits me. Darnit! I ate a whole bag of chips while watching *American Idol* last night. I say to myself with frustration, "Shoot! I wasn't going to do that! NO, no, no, you've been doing so good!" But... I did it anyway. It started with just one, then a small handful at the next commercial break. The urge kept escalating, and my mind was yelling, "Just eat the bag, who cares!"

Now this morning after the impulse has passed, I wonder, "How did I get to that point? OMG! I blew it!" Left with guilt, remorse and frustration, the truth is, I'm starting over...again.

That girl used to be me. I would be twenty pounds up, then fifteen down. Forty pounds back on, and twenty off. If there was a movie headline that described my life, it would have been called:

Courage... Fit Mindset Now... and Self Love!

This picture is a selection of MBFC girls from across the United States. These women are remarkable! All of them showed up to their lives, and are living fit now. They agreed to take this picture in their undies to show they are courageous in their effort to shed weight on this 'mind-body-spirit' weight-loss journey with girlfriends. Some have lost 5 pounds, others 25 and 40. One girl in this picture has lost 105 pounds! They are all Fit Chicks no matter where they are in their journey, because a MBFC Fit Chick is a state of mind, not a number on the scale. Read what they have learned about themselves by embracing weight loss from this new perspective.

Wendy: Self Confidence is about your mind, not your body!

Diane: I surround myself with friends that are positive and inspiring.

Marcia: I am a wonderful, beautiful woman...that I am.

Carol: Changing my inner voice changes my outer person for the better.

Lupita: I am assertive, beautiful, courageous, energetic and healthy!

Linda: I have a warrior within me.

Lisa: Taking care of myself is not a luxury; I owe it to myself.

Genelle: I have done 5 half marathons and 5 triathlons in this body. I love inspiring other women.

Jaylene: I finally found my inner fit chick!

MBFC Girls

Burn Your Fat Pants: Candid Guidance from a Girlfriend

Chapter 1

Because You Matter

The starting point of great success and achievement has always been the same.
It is for you to dream big dreams.
—Brian Tracy

Heavy Exhalation...

Constant flippn' attention to my eating habits is so much work. It's much easier to just get over it and live with the fact that I am NOT, and never will be, little miss hot body. But dangit, at the same time, it's just so frustrating because I do want to be thinner and look my best!

Is this where you are with your weight frustrations? Sista, I hear **YOU**!

Most definitely, you are due for a fresh perspective. It's important to remember why you have chosen this weight loss journey. 'Cause girl, it is definitely a choice. At times it may seem much easier to go back to your old way of doing things; less work and fewer personal commitments, but just because it becomes difficult doesn't mean you should give up on your goal of having a fit, lean body. Let me remind you of why you would want to stick with creating this new lifestyle. **It's because YOU matter.**

Imagine visiting the park for a day of picnicking and relaxation in the warm afternoon sun. After parking the car, you follow a winding dirt trail through a dry, rocky landscape knowing there must be lush ground ahead. The search is on for the perfect scenic spot. As you venture down the trail you are greeted with a flourishing canyon of picturesque rock and wildflowers. From where you stand, the surroundings are rugged, yet just across the canyon are blooming hillsides, and tall swaying trees. As you gaze across the gorge you notice a flat, grassy area alongside the river's edge. It's the perfect lunching spot. Your eyes begin to scout for a bridge or rocks to traverse the river. With excitement to get to the other side, you think, "There must be a way." And with determination you set off to find a crossing.

The gap between the harsh, unforgiving land and the inviting picnic spot is where the true journey lies. You must navigate your way to cross over from the years of battling weight to a lifestyle of loving yourself more. The opportunity is before you, and it matters that you cross the rocks to the other side. All you have to do is make the decision. Decide that however difficult the passage may be, the trip will be worth your efforts. Your picnic will be that much more enjoyable because of the fact that it is in a location that is less traveled, a place you can call your own secret sanctuary.

To enjoy the best life possible, you must take care of your fitness health. Your dreams, aspirations, and relationships are all compromised if you don't. This includes your emotional and mental health as well. In an article published by Scientific American, it is noted that vigorous physical exercise is critical to mental health. So, although fitting into skinny jeans may be an awesome feeling and a target to shoot for; it's not just about aesthetics. There must be a deeper vision.

Untrue Truths

There are women that use their bodies as a means to hide. They have learned to believe they are incapable of enjoying certain experiences in life because of their

Exercise makes you happier!

weight. The *Joie de Vivre*—a French phrase for the "Joys of Life"—may not be fully expressed simply because they live in an overweight body.

Some women I speak with are so unhappy with their bodies that they stop having sex. They don't think they are as sexy as they once were, and feel uncomfortable being naked. They are insecure with their bodies, and make up beliefs about what their partners think of them. Often those beliefs are unfounded, yet they allow their own feelings about their body to skew their judgment, and a communication breakdown drives a wedge between the couple. If you've been a culprit in this limiting belief, you've done both your partner and yourself a colossal disservice.

Other women stop being active once they've aged, and/or gained weight. They forget what it was like to be young and full of energy. The old bike collects spider webs in the garage, and the treadmill becomes a dumping ground for the ironing. Even middleaged Moms cease playing with their children in a physical way, and limit themselves just to the non-moving activities—books, cooking, and crafts. They let Dad do the physical stuff.

I once took my two children to a park while on a business trip in Ohio. When we arrived at the playground, I observed a group of five or more Moms sitting on the park bench engaging in conversation with each other and eating McDonalds while their kids played on the equipment. Because of my heightened awareness in working with weight issues, I also noticed all the Moms were overweight.

I went on with my purpose for visiting the park, and started a game of **tag the tree** with my kids. Before long we had all the other children playing with us too. We had about a dozen kids running from tree to tree, counting off as they tagged the tree, and running to the next one. It was fun; I got my exercise and they did too! I probably burned off the amount of calories that the Moms on the bench had consumed.

The only difference between those Moms and me is, I have a different mindset. The Moms overlooked their options while at the park. They could have gotten off the bench; smiled, laughed and played with their kids, but they didn't exercise their opportunity. Imagine how much fun the kids would have had with Mom? And think about the opportunity she could have given them to live by example?

There are those gals, and perhaps you're one of them that is driven, striving for your goals despite a weight issue. Our Mind Body Fit Club friend June has said, "Weight becomes the big elephant in the room." Conquering goals, making the deadlines, and achieving success, yet doing so with a lack of achievement in one major area of life—your health. Whatever your deal is, your weight is affecting your performance in life. **Your health matters, because YOU matter.**

The real deal, and the reason I am reaching out to you is much deeper than a diet. I believe you have the right to live in the healthiest, most beautiful body possible for you. I also am with the strongest conviction that your body is an interpretation of what's going on in your head. Drawing from my experience as a Hypnotherapist, I can safely say **you are what you have believed you are.**

For many years, I lived my life thinking, and doing things from a mediocre existence. Although I spent much of my alone time dreaming about a life of grandeur, my reality was nothing of the sort. Then, at the age of twenty four, I met a guy...

A friend called and said she wanted to set me up with her boyfriend's cousin. I asked, as any girl does, "Well, what's he like?" She answered, "He's kinda short, balding, and hairy, but he's really funny!" I thought, hardly my knight in shining armor, but the funny part intrigued me.

As it turned out, he was a comedy stage Hypnotist. And, he was really funny! It was never a dull moment with this guy. He made me laugh, and you know as well as I do, we like that quality in a man, right? We hit it off and became fast friends. Like a rock star groupie, I had fun attending his audience-packed Hypnosis shows.

Within just months of dating, and hanging out at his performances, one night his stage assistant abruptly quit the show. She had played the part of the Vanna White of Hypnosis; assisting the Hypnotist with sound cues, props, and looking pretty in her dazzling dress of the evening. Next thing I know, I am being cleverly persuaded into her position. I willingly accepted the opportunity with the idea that it would be exciting to travel, have more laughs, and live a lifestyle that seemed full of fun. But to be on stage? Yikes! Part of me wanted to be that girl, but another part did not feel worthy of such a status.

I felt like the audience would see right through my façade. I could be up on stage acting confident, but it was truly just an act. At the time, I had little direction in my life. I was in a vicious cycle of uncertainty; yo-yo dieting, struggling with bouts of childhood drama, and dealing with a wrath of low self-esteem issues.

I could stand up there on stage playing the part, but when it came to speaking in front of the audience, that was another playing field. I had little confidence, and the belief that I had nothing to say. Night after night, as part of my stage duties, I had to announce the star Hypnotist as he came on to the stage. I wanted to die every time. In fact, did you know? Statistics show that more people would rather die than speak publicly? Yep, I was in that category. Maybe you are too? I would actually hide in order to get the job done. I was the invisible voice behind the curtain.

After two years together, and literally thousands of shows around the world, we parted ways. From that relationship, I have many adventurous and very funny memories. I also gained tremendous stage experience, and valuable insight into the world of Hypnosis. Little did I realize, that boyfriend had given me more than just an opportunity to travel the world, he led me to a future career, and a path to finding myself.

Soon after we went our separate directions, I found myself contemplating with a friend on what I should do for a job. I questioned my future? Should I go back to what I was doing before my whirlwind Hypnosis experience? Makeup artistry and cosmetology had been my field of choice, but somehow it seemed dull in comparison.

My friend said, "De'Anna, you should be a Hypnotist." We laughed over that novel idea. After all, I was terrified of the microphone, and shivered at the thought of speaking in front of people. There was no way that could work. I had done my assistant job well, but being the one in front was something I could not fathom.

That same afternoon, after talking with my friend, I went to the gym. After my workout, I thumbed through the newspaper in the lobby searching for a fun weekend event to attend. As I turned the page, an advertisement jumped from the page shouting Hypnotherapy Training. It really did feel like a shout, as if it were a sign from God, or a blinking Vegas style neon light. My friend and I had just been laughing about me being a Hypnotist, and here it was in black and white, an opportunity shouting in my face.

I decided, perhaps for the first time in life, to follow through. I signed up to further my training in Hypnosis. Thank goodness I made that decision, for it would become a defining moment in my life. I have later realized that all of the very necessary, and sometimes, not fun series of events with that boyfriend lead me to the place that began my healing. (Thank you, you know who you are.)

In hypnotherapy training, we spent many hours in class hypnotizing each other for practice. Each day there would be individuals, myself included, leaving class in tears and feeling like a total mess. Imagine spending your entire day, days on end in therapy? It was like cleaning out the stored crap in your house. It's a frustrating, often overwhelming, and very dirty job. But once you do it, you feel free and elated.

With formal Hypnosis training in hand, it was time to confront my next hurdle. I thought I needed to be a size six to get on stage to perform a comedy Hypnosis show. I didn't think people would want to look at a chunky girl with a microphone. I kept thinking, "I need to lose weight. I need to be good on my diet." But as I continued to peel back the layers of my own emotional issues with hypnotherapy sessions, I realized that I was using my extra weight as an excuse to never truly achieve my goals. It was my way of staying comfortable; my way of having a reason as to why I can't pursue more in my life. I had not lived up to my full potential thus far. So, taking the back seat was, once again, my mediocre thinking coming to fruition. I was used to sitting in the back seat, and not fully engaging in my unused abilities.

I intuitively knew that to be successful on stage I had to go do it. There was no room for toying with the idea. I had performed thousands of shows with my previous experience, and I was growing quite tired of sabotaging myself. It was now or never. I needed to trust my instinct, and flail myself out there.

With a greater vision, I did just that; I performed my very first show on my own. It was terrifying and exhilarating at the same time. In the car, on the way home from the gig, I said with relief "I never have to do my first show again... It's all good from here on out." Performing that show in a body I didn't love, risking the embarrassment, and doing it anyway was the first time I felt truly empowered. The day after that show was the first day of the rest of my life as a self assured woman. It didn't happen all at once, but a gradual process to uncovering the real me.

I later married the love of my life, and we have been together for over ten years now. He and I met back in those first days of going through hypnotherapy training. He loved me as the chunky girl with the false confidence, and has watched me grow into a whole woman.

Together we developed, produced and performed comedy Hypnosis shows all over the United States and overseas. Miraculously, the extra weight that I had been gaining and losing for so many years started to come off. For the very first time, I wasn't even trying to lose weight. I was simply standing in my own power.

After the first season of traveling on the road performing (about 5 months), I returned to California several sizes smaller. I had shed weight naturally by actively being courageous. I had stepped out of my comfort zone, and leaped beyond the old self esteem issues. That leap paid off! It has provided me with an amazing career, a path to discovering my own hidden talents, a wonderful sense of self, and a powerful tool that I get to share with you.

Have you taken a back seat to your true potential?

Do you use your weight as an excuse?

I know what it's like to be in the darkness of unworthiness. I also know what it's like to stand in front of ten thousand people speaking, performing and having so much fun living what feels like a dream. Over the years I have performed for Governors, Five Star Generals, opened for top musical acts, and Fortune 500 companies. I have stood in moments that I once dreamt about as a little girl. I knew by the age of eight that I wanted to be a performer. I could visualize myself up on the stage smiling and dancing in a big way. Then life happened, and I let my negative experiences hinder my dreams, and skew my worthiness. It wasn't until I took responsibility for the life that I created that it began to change into the life I wanted.

Your Significance

Do you feel significant to the world? Do you feel like you matter to the people around you? These are important questions to ask yourself, but the answer is not an external one. The answer must come from within you. You cannot measure your significance by what others think, say or even credit you.

You have to care about yourself enough to get your butt off the couch. That's step one. Despite over-scheduling, and a multitude of priorities, it's your responsibility to show the world around you that you care enough about yourself to make living healthy a significant part of your life.

You, and only you, are responsible for etching out a life that you can feel good about. Your significance in the world can only be measured by how you feel about yourself. When you know you've done the things you said you would do, when you've been the example of what you want your kids to be, and when you've struggled and persevered, then you can feel peace within knowing that your life matters.

To do this, you've got to reach for what you want. As much as a Mom wants her baby to walk, she can't do it for her. I can remember being on the floor with my little one saying, "Come on, you can do it", as she struggled to make all her limbs move harmoniously together. She'd flop on her belly, take an accidental nose dive towards the carpet, or roll over. It was most definitely a feat she was tenacious to figure out. Her determination was innate. She didn't sit around thinking, Oh I can't because of this or that, she just kept at it until she completed the task; each time learning a little more of what to do and what not to do. I could help by holding out my fingers, encourage her with my words, but the act of walking had to be done all on her own.

This weight loss journey is an act you must figure out. You've spent way too much time feeling bamboozled, lost and defeated. Now is your time to bring forth the realization that the choices you make, and how you take care of your health is significant in your world.

Your life matters. How you spend your time, and the impact you choose to make in your life makes a difference. You may have unique talents that are untapped, and dormant. I believe hiding your personal gifts is a disfavor to your life. Would you advise a budding young woman to NOT use her talents; hindering her growth and personal development? Of course you wouldn't!

Imagine having wonderful gifts wrapped up beautifully under the Christmas tree, and never opening them. I encourage you to take off the wrapping, expose the gift inside and put it to good use! You may very well have strengths and abilities that perhaps you never realized would be so useful to your weight loss journey.

Perhaps you are a great cook. If you learned to transform your favorite dishes into healthy delicious meals you could be an asset to your friends, neighbors and family that are struggling to eat right. Heck, you could even be the next healthy cooking star on the Food Network.

Maybe you are a natural leader but you are leading your friends in the wrong direction getting together for Martini night, rather than a brisk walk around the neighborhood. You could utilize your leadership skills to rally your friends in joining you for an accountability get together once a week, or even lead your friends in training for a women's 10K to support a good cause.

The time is now for a mind awakening. Every woman in the universe has some unique quality that can be the missing piece to her weight loss puzzle. The only way to discover your inner resources is to interact with your feelings, thoughts and aspirations. It's time to dream again!

This weight-loss journey that you take with me will be from a much different perspective than what you've grown accustomed to with dieting. I'm going to ask you to discover your passion for life, and use it as a catalyst to help you conquer your struggle with extra weight. If you don't know what you're passionate about, that's great too. I guarantee this process will help you to get closely connected with your insides, so that your outside becomes a new reflection of YOU.

Soon you could be living a life free from stressing about fitting into your clothes, free from talking about what diet you're on, and free from worrying about gaining weight at the holidays; no longer loving yourself with food, or using food as your favorite pastime saying, "I don't know why, I just love to eat!"

Along my journey to becoming fit, I learned that food will never feed me like self worth will. I have simply taken care of the emotional eating behaviors that once imprisoned me, and adopted a new mindset. I still have challenges, we all do. It's called Life. Yet I feel equipped to overcome those challenges by practicing the strategies that I will share with you in this book.

My hope is for you to discover your own "OMG moments" (Oh My Gosh, I can't believe I have been doing that to myself?). Trust that you have this information in your hands because it is the right time. I ask that you accept the challenge to get honest with yourself, and have the courage to uncover what you have stuffed down inside.

I discovered that I'm worth the effort it takes to better myself. I know you're worth it too. Are you ready to discover the body and life of your dreams? Are you ready to believe in yourself? It's never too late.

In the next chapter, you'll learn the attitude that will explosively start your journey to getting the results you want. Be willing to open your mind to new ideas and perceptions. Let's go friend! Jump with me on a leap of faith...

I matter
to the world around me.

Burn Your Fat Pants: Candid Guidance from a Girlfriend

F.I.T. Strategy Exercise

Because I Matter

Sit down with paper and pen. Close your eyes.
Ask yourself, with your health and body in mind:

Why am I Important?...

I'm passionate
I'm creative
I'm a thinker
I'm there for people
I matter.

Because I Matter

Burn Your Fat Pants: Candid Guidance from a Girlfriend

Chapter 2

Willingness

No one is in control of your happiness but you, therefore, you have the power to change anything about yourself or your life that you want to change.

— Barbara de Angelis

I like to think of being willing as a cheerful agreement with yourself. When you are willing, you are in a state of continuous flowing growth. It is a non-judgmental, and an ever-evolving state of mind. You are not reluctant. You are optimistic, excited about the possibilities of the future, and eager to learn.

Willingness is readiness; showing up to your life, and being ready for anything that comes your way. You have to be willing to do what other people are not in order to achieve weight loss success. You have to be willing to take the necessary steps to overcome any obstacle that enters your path. That, is true willingness.

I ask you...

What are you willing to change in order to have a fit, lean body? What are you willing to sacrifice?

Perhaps you're thinking, "Whoooaaa! Wait a minute De'Anna, that's all too much!" And you are right. It is too much all at once. Let me lift your worries. All you really have to do at this point in the process is be willing to believe there is a way to your goal outside of dieting.

The Closed Mind, the Importance of Love and Cleaning House

Many times a woman with a closed mind doesn't even recognize herself to be this way. Perhaps she is a volunteer for her daughter's Brownie Troop, or a leader amongst her peers in her industry. She is visibly present in activities, but when it comes to her personal issues, she's closed off.

The woman with a closed mind is rigid and inflexible; no longer receiving, or growing. She builds emotional walls and chooses to live life disconnected from herself; as if she can remain anonymous there. Her walls act as a shield, protecting her from that in which she is not ready to manage. Within this lonely existence she remains fragile and broken, just wanting to be accepted, and loved. She may say she wants to lose weight, but is unwilling to face her fears, and insecurities.

The most disappointing aspect of a woman unwilling to believe in herself, is that she doesn't have to be this way. It truly comes down to the fundamental need for unconditional love. No matter your stature or position in life, not one of us is exempt from it. We all seek love and acceptance.

I once guided a Hypnosis session whereas my client was a very powerful CEO. The ability to achieve great financial success was a focus she conquered having made millions of dollars in her career. Unbeknownst to the outside world, she felt alone and unloved on the inside.

Our session revealed a childhood of abandonment and fear. Although as an adult, she had obtained what many strive for in life, she still felt incomplete. Great financial success was the one thing that temporarily filled that void. But what she was truly after, was love.

Be an Inspiring Friend!

Burn Your Fat Pants: Candid Guidance from a Girlfriend

While you read through these pages, I am asking you to be willing to delve into the process of discovering your unconditional self love. The distance between where you are now, and where you imagine yourself to be at your ideal weight starts with a willing attitude. As you embark on this journey, you'll find that inspiration is all around you. By reaching out, and being willing to admit that you could use some guidance, you will create an energy shift in the way that you shine in the world. All that you need to guide you will show up in your life.

In the Mind Body Fit Club, we have a courageous woman whose name is Marcia. She's in her mid-fifties and exemplifies this trait to great extent. She's lost almost twenty inches since being involved in the Mind Body Fit Club program, and has gone from a size 18 to a size 12 so far. We have watched her transform into the most energetic, inspired fitness enthusiast Ohio has ever seen.

She is involved in softball, bowling, and religiously attends her favorite Zumba class. She is so pumped with exuberance that she even slides head first into home base during her softball games. **Again, she's in her fifties!** She is willing to lay it all on the line for her team. The motivation she has created, comes from within, and is attractive to all that know her. She even prides herself on how much dirt she comes home with on her jersey. Our Mind Body Fit Club girls now use the phrase, **"I Eat Dirt!"** in honor of her contagious energy.

Her enthusiasm has not come from a life without toil. She has experienced her share of heartbreak and self doubt. She was once in a bad, first marriage, and repeatedly told she was worthless and stupid.

The memories of those years still create a feeling of sadness, knowing now that she had a choice. She's come a long way since those days. Through personal growth and healing, she now chooses to live her life inspired. She's even married to the man of her dreams that is supportive and loving.

This weight loss journey is about acknowledging your whole self. You must adopt a willing approach to life; become a student that is ever evolving. That may require you to be willing to risk being hurt, be willing to stand up for yourself or take a chance on letting people see the real you.

 It may entail sifting through the old emotional crap that seems to be a re-occurring theme in your life. Your body has been holding on to all of it, like the junk drawer in your kitchen. Are you willing to sort through it?

We've all seen the TV shows that help families get rid of their junk. The experts come in to their unorganized existence, and facilitate a transformation by quickly examining each item, then categorizing it into sections.

They create three categories. Save. Trash. Give away. After days of sifting through the years of piles, and junk, the end result leaves the homeowner feeling uplifted, and free to start a new life.

In this weight loss process you will SAVE your talents, abilities, strengths, self esteem and confidence. TRASH the old excuses, pity parties, negative mindsets and beliefs. And GIVE AWAY the habits and junk foods that are not supporting your goals. In the end, you too will have an amazing feeling of freedom! Let's back

Enthusiasm is Contagious!

up for moment. For this process to be successful...you must start by being willing.

I believe, let me re-phrase that, I know, that you are much more capable than you think you are. We have incorporated fitness events into our programs as a regular practice because participating in them builds personal confidence and belief. Walking or jogging your first 5 or 10K will inspire you to believe in yourself. Not only do you prove to yourself that you CAN do it, but often, you prove that you could probably go even farther! You wouldn't have believed it, if you hadn't actually done it yourself.

"The spirit indeed is willing, but the flesh is weak." You cannot lose weight through the tasks of the body alone, you must engage your spirit; the deeper more powerful part of you. The quote mentioned comes from biblical times, so you see this is not a new concept, but indeed a new method for you to shed weight.

A state of willingness empowers you to let go of all the old excuses. In regards to overcoming habituated patterns, Dr. Wayne Dyer states in his bestselling book *Excuses Be Gone*, "You'll ultimately realize that there are no excuses worth defending, ever, even if they've always been part of your life."

You may be creating excuses that seem legit, but they are not. There are a group of co-workers at a friend's company that get together to walk at lunchtime. They are varied shapes and sizes, and mostly women. One of the heaviest women in the group creates constant conversation of how she wants to drop a few pounds, yet she often announces that once again she has forgotten her walking shoes at home. One of the other women finally told her to buy two pairs of shoes. One pair to keep at home and another to keep at the office so that she wouldn't need to use that excuse anymore.

I am excited to share with you valuable insights in the next section. You will have a better understanding of why you do what you do, and how to overcome the limitations that have held you back. Come with me.....I'll help you find your courage.

I am willing to commit to myself on a deeper level.

F.I.T. Strategy Exercise

Willingness

Write out the excuses you use to avoid eating better, exercising at your peak performance or as limiting factors to your success at losing weight.

Close your eyes first, and ask your inner mind to recall all the excuses you have allowed yourself to entertain. Write down even those that feel legitimate. With a timer set to five minutes, take in a deep breath...then let your mind and pen fly!

1 Back injury
2 "I don't feel like it"
3 It's too difficult for me
4 I like food too much
5... Deadlines ("It's too close to Christmas/Birthday/etc")

Chapter 3

Understanding YOU

Nothing makes a woman more beautiful than the belief that she is beautiful.
—Sophia Loren

It's not entirely your fault that you're overweight. Are you agreeing, shaking your head yes, thinking "Yeah, it's my job, it's so stressful", or "I know it's not my fault, my husband eats crappy food and it's such a bad influence on me."

Uhhhh....girlfriend, pull your head out. I apologize for having to be so forward, but those are just excuses; symptoms of the real issue. Your job is not the reason you are overweight. When I state that it's not your fault that you are overweight, I am referring to the origin of your beliefs and behaviors.

You have been programmed by your life experiences. As a young child you were very receptive, and impressionable. You had not yet developed critical factoring, and therefore you simply took in information, like a sponge. Anyone who had a direct influence in your life—parents, family members, teachers, pastors, and others—constantly conveyed information that you collected unconsciously. It was during this period of early growth that your lifelong belief systems were developed, and behavioral patterns began to grow and mold. Situations, experiences, people, and words made an impression on you. How you handle your life now is made up from all of that collective information.

Think about the word *impression*, and what it means. The dictionary describes:

Impression: a mark, or imprint. An effect produced, as on the mind or senses, by some force or influence.

A Mind Body Fit Club member shared, when she was a young girl her mother took her to the Diet Center, a chain of weight loss centers in business in the eighties. She walked from the car observing the sign on the building wondering why they were going there. Before she knew it, she was signed up and being told to eat a selection of their packaged foods. She recalls thinking that her Mom felt the Diet Center would help her. Yet, she had been unaware there was a problem until then. This sent strong messages of inadequacy. She says she remembers thinking, "If I could be skinnier, my Mom will love me more."

This scenario truly exemplifies how the adults that reared us held great responsibility in influencing our belief systems. Our subconscious minds are shaped and molded by those who have had persuasive influence upon us as children.

Every impressionable experience of your life has left a mark or imprint within your subconscious mind. Those imprints cause that familiar voice in your head to speak positively or negatively to you. Have you ever said?

"I can't do it."

"I've already blown it, I might as well eat the whole thing now."

"I don't have time to exercise, I'm too busy."

"Just this one brownie"

"As I age, I keep gaining weight."

"Screw it, I'm fat anyway"

The list goes on and on, and so do the imprints. Many of those words in your head are not even your own. How many times have you said something and as

Love the 'lil girl inside of you!

it falls out of your mouth, you realize you sound just like your mother or your father. Ah Hah! You have an imprint.

Your history can also influence you in positive ways, and perhaps you love that you have taken on certain characteristics from your rearing. That's a really great thing! That is what we strive for as parents. But it doesn't always happen that way. Sometimes the opinions of others were strong, and miscommunicated. The original intention may have been positive, but as the message flowed downstream into your little mind, it was received as something entirely different. Often with the filter of, "I must not be good enough."

I know for sure that I want to be my own woman, expressing myself from my personal beliefs and values. Not a parrot repeating what I've been told, or a puppet dancing a jig from another person's decisions. I believe that is how I have become a whole woman; by sorting through the opinions of others, the labels put on me as a child, and deciding for myself who I am.

Wouldn't you like your beliefs to be your own, and not adopted from someone else? This weight loss process can be an empowering and life changing experience that gives you the ability to design your own life. I am hopeful you are wrapping your brain around this information right now, because it's a POTENT idea.

In his parable book, *The Ant and the Elephant*, respected author and Olympian Vince Poscente explains the relationship between the conscious, and the subconscious mind, in my opinion, more simply and beautifully than anyone. He tells the story of Adir and Elgo both searching for meaning in their lives, and how they found hope and success in finding each other.

The ant represents the conscious mind, and the elephant, the mighty and powerful subconscious. The little ant spends his whole life on a relentless journey to find the promise land, when he shockingly discovers his life's pursuit has been spent on the back of the elephant. It's a good read, and I highly recommend spending a quick two hours with it. It gives a metaphoric understanding of how the conscious and subconscious minds work together. We often spend so much time thinking it's our will-power that needs to change, while all along a much greater power is keeping us from achieving our goal.

You see, your mind is like a computer. The conscious mind is much like you sitting at your desk manipulating the software, and information in your computer. You decipher facts, add and delete, think in black and white, and make decisions based on the stored information. While your subconscious is like the hard drive. It does not analyze the information; it simply stores the content.

Imagine the hard drive content is all of your life experiences. Perhaps you experienced a controlling mother, or an abusive parent or family member—sexual, physical, emotional or otherwise. Maybe you had lack of a parent altogether, and experienced the hardships of that reality. From the lows of childhood trauma, to the highs of achievement throughout your rearing, both good and bad, all of it made an impression, and it is the stored data in your hard drive.

The information and experiences that are stored in the subconscious mind, or your hard drive, have formed the foundation of your belief systems. These belief systems either propel you forward, or they hold you back.

When I was growing up I often heard the statement, "There are children starving in China. Eat everything on your plate. You cannot get up from the table until your plate is clean." Those words became engrained in my mind, and formed a powerful habit for me, finishing everything on my plate, always. As an adult this habit greatly contributed to over-eating, which lead to weight gain. It's been a habit that is hard to shake loose simply because those words are an impression infused upon the walls of my mind. Can you relate?

Think about how powerful this concept is to your weight loss. My belief that I needed to eat everything on my plate was a message in my subconscious. It was my stored data. In my adult life, I knew that eating smaller meals, or stopping when I was full was the correct way to eat healthy. Yet, I found it very difficult to do, because my computer had old programming. For years, I had let my Mother's beliefs become mine. Not intentionally, but subconsciously.

A client, we'll call her Janie for confidentiality sake, once said to me, "I can't lose weight. Everything I have tried just does not work. When I do lose, I gain it back. I guess I am destined to be fat just like my Mom, my Aunts, and my sisters. It's just our body type." Her words came from what she believed to be her truth, and her truth became her inability to lose weight no matter what diet she tried.

It's as if she sat down at her desk, and typed into her computer on Sunday-

This week's To Do List:

1. Start Diet on Monday

2. Exercise daily...

3. Eat more vegetables

But, when she starts her diet on Monday, all of the stored content in the hard drive, her limiting belief systems and past failures now come into play mode and sabotage her diet soon thereafter. The will-power to say no to sabotaging foods is just not enough. She feels discouraged when she blows it, and Janie believes she just can't do it, giving even more truth to her already limited belief about herself.

But it's not Janie's fault, after all, she is merely working off of the information that is accessible to her. She is deriving from her existing hard drive. What is the definition of insanity? Doing the same thing over and over and expecting a different result. She cannot expect to change her outcome, unless she switches out the stored content on her hard drive. Janie needs new programming.

When I was growing up, my Mother and I had a tumultuous relationship. I now believe that it was a result of my parents divorcing at an early age. My Mom was very angry and hurt by the divorce, and her emotions spilled over to my four year old receptive mind. Therefore, I became angry too. My resentful emotions were never directed towards my Dad, but always like a boomerang of fury back at Mom. I did not feel like I had an outlet to express that rage, so my Mom often received the brunt of it.

In addition, Mom found it difficult to say I love you. Not just to me, but in general, and to all four of us kids. One can only guess that her inability to express her love verbally was derived from the way she was raised and her own hurts and pains. But never-the-less, I was a kid, and like all kids, I needed to be loved.

Although she did not say the words I love you, Mom did however express her love for us through baking. Just about every day, I would come home from school, and be greeted by the smell of fresh baked chocolate brownies, chocolate chip cookies, lemon bars, or angel food cakes. It was like walking into a giant hug. It was her way of saying I love you. Ahhh...the warmth of yummy treats for my tummy. Food instantly stimulates the senses. My receptors were open, and storing the data. It wasn't long before I registered that food meant love. It was the easiest, fastest, most convenient way to self soothe.

Kids need love, and I (snickering) loved myself often with food. My sister and I were eager to take on this baking love as well. We often pulled out all the ingredients for made-from-scratch chocolate chip cookies. But our cookie dough almost never made it to the oven. We'd eat the batter from the metal bowl by finger lick and spoonful until it was gone. We'd feel sick having ingested the unbaked cookies, but we'd do it again, time after time.

I obviously didn't consciously realize these behaviors were being formed, otherwise I wouldn't have participated in a process that would cause so many years of grief. But this is the point. Our subconscious is powerful.

Thinking back over those younger years, I have realized my world was forming around me, and I was being molded by the unconscious data being collected. My belief systems were being shaped by how I perceived my family to feel about me. My friends, my circumstances, and my decisions were based on how I believed I fit into my world. There is a lot of room for error in that process. Many truths were not true at all, yet I perceived them to be my reality.

For me, food was not just for the basic need of keeping my body alive. It meant much more than that; it was a life-line. It became part of me, and how I dealt with situations. As the years went by, I continued to use food for emotional stability. It wouldn't be until I was thirty years old that I made the connection...I don't have to use food for love, I can just love myself.

Finally, as an adult woman, Ding, Ding, Ding...bells are ringing, trumpets are blaring, light bulbs are blinking...Holy Cow, it was as if a veil had been lifted, and I could now see the light!

Here is where the real work begins...

I encourage you to take a moment to examine your belief systems, and the old programming that might be playing in your head? Your story may be very different from mine, but it's a sure bet that your current behaviors have roots that are long and embedded.

At the end of this, and every chapter you may have already discovered, there is opportunity to engage in the process of rewriting your hard drive with the F.I.T. Session Exercises. I believe it is absolutely imperative that you make important mental shifts to your subconscious in order to yield more positive results than you've been getting. We must recondition the mind to perceive a new you.

Think about how your history has developed your beliefs about yourself. How have life's influences over the years contributed to your body image, self esteem, and eating habits? What were your parent's opinions, habits and beliefs?

You are holding the key in what's been keeping you from being successful in losing weight permanently. Remember the three critical components that I referred to in the Introduction? Smaller meals, regular exercise, and behavior change. As a whole, they are the essential ingredients to your success. It's not just about exercising your ass off like the biggest losers, or depriving yourself of your favorite foods for weeks on end. It's more than that.

Anyone who has ever successfully dieted, and actually **kept the weight off for good** has succeeded in all three areas. It was not the diet that helped them achieve their goal, it was the fact that they changed their belief systems as they also made better food choices, and created a schedule of regular exercise. They changed their old habits, and formed a healthy, new lifestyle.

Are you ready to face your inner belief systems, and shift them towards your highest good? If you said "Yes!"... let's get started.

You must decide right now what your standards are for yourself. It is imperative that you begin to raise your bar. You must make YOU a priority in your life, and begin to feel worthy of the time you spend with yourself. You must also start caring about what and how much you eat, not because you're on a diet, but because YOU MATTER, and your health matters.

Science proves that to have lasting results at anything, a shift in consciousness must occur. In other words, it is vital that you revisit the issue from a different state of consciousness than the one that created it. So if you've had a weight issue, and I imagine that is why you're reading this book, then you must do things differently than you've always done, in order to have new desired results. **You must re-create your habits, and begin to live your life as who you want to be, rather than who you've been.** Read that last line again, it's vital to your success. You must load new software in your hard drive.

I'm going to be super, straight-up honest with you. I have good news, and I have bad news.

The good news is, you're not the same person today that created the original bad habits that you've been working against. Remember at the beginning of this chapter, I stated, it's not really even your fault that you're still overweight? You've just been working with the same old programming, the old hard data facts that predict the same results over and over. It's no wonder you're so frustrated, and at your wits end with weight loss!

Your subconscious mind has done its job well. It has carried out its duty to override any fleeting act of "I'm going to be good with what I eat this week". Your subconscious hard drive knows better, and is ready to kick in with its powerful old programming. Your subconscious mind, your 90% power, is running off of the negative belief systems that are installed; the belief systems that your life experience has created for you. The life experiences that have been derived, not just from childhood, but all the other impressionable moments; divorce, death, trauma, bad relationships, embarrassment, lack of worthiness and more. And that is the good news! You might be saying, "What? I don't follow, that's the good news?" Stay with me, you'll soon GET IT, I promise...

Let's get on to the bad news. The bad news is, this is not going to happen overnight. I'm not going to tell you that you can lose 40 pounds in 4 weeks and keep it off. That's ridiculous! I refuse to be dishonest with you, and stoop to the level of the liars in the diet business. The highway billboards and TV commercials are full of empty promises that will only keep you spending your money, and sabotaging your long-term success.

This is going to require your full attention, and it's going to be totally worth it. Why? Because you're worth it. It may be the most challenging thing you have ever experienced in your life. This process may send you into a full spectrum of emotions finding yourself one day in a pity of tears, and another at the breakthrough of victory. **You are required to start feeling with your soul *rather* than your stomach.** It's high time you acknowledge yourself as worthy of having the body you want.

There may be moments through this process that you feel like you are hanging out of an airplane without a chute. And that will be great, because it means that you are being pushed from your comfort zone of doing what you've always done. In those moments, you are re-writing your hard drive. It will be worth your courage! So you see... it really is all **Good News**!

Perhaps you are a person that doesn't even know where to begin with losing weight. You've tried all the diets, and you're still back at square one. It's discouraging, you're confused, and you're tired. Maybe some days you have an inkling of motivation, but it just feels too hard, and too time consuming to devote your life to weight loss. You may even be a woman that's never even tried to diet, because you've resolved that you are simply built a certain way. Well ladies, I am here to declare, **the body you want is developed from the inside out**.

The reason it has felt like such a battle is because it is. You're up against that powerful machine we've been chatting about—your subconscious mind. If you don't have it working for you, then it will surely take control, and work against you. It is up to you now to delete the old bad habits, emotions, and behaviors that do not serve you. You must input new information and resources, and deposit so much good stuff into your mind that you begin taking action in new ways, and replacing the old thinking with a new powerful YOU.

Decide now that you are devoting your mind, body and soul to this process. It doesn't mean that getting slim will have to take 100% of your time. It does mean however that you must devote yourself in a new **way. You've got to commit on**

a deeper level. This process is not about pussy-footing around with eating healthier, and dabbling in more exercise, and saying you're on a diet. BULLS*%T! This is like boot camp for your inner behaviors. You've got to step it up, and believe in YOU. Trust yourself through this process, and let's get to the ROOT so that you never have to diet again.

Are ya with me, girl? Good, let's do it together. I've got your back. I've done this myself, and write from my own experience. Even if you don't believe me yet, I know as your coach that...YOU GOT THIS!

Chapter Four offers up important mindset techniques to your continued journey. You'll learn **why** you have been stuck in diet cycles, and how to adopt the mindset and behaviors that will align you with living as a Fit Chick. You are only pages away from information that could shift your thinking from this moment forward.

Today, I choose to re-write my programming and future experiences.

Burn Your Fat Pants: Candid Guidance from a Girlfriend

F.I.T. Strategy Exercise

Understanding Me

This exercise will help you to recall your stored data. It is important that you bring the information that is filed through visualizations, feeling, and memory to the screen of your mind. Close your eyes, and ask your inner mind to access the associations you have regarding your history with food and body image. It is important that you put pen to paper, and let your hand express words through the thoughts that instantly come to your mind. This is not a time to analyze; it is an opportunity to express...

My History

I turn to food because I am depressed. I have developed depression after years of frustration in my relationship with my mother. She is controlling, and her actions have led me to believe I can't be trusted. I can't make my own decisions. I was always fat, she says. I remember. Dad was yes, mom was no, every time. This kind of denial made me feel restricted. I felt unfree. Every time these emotions surfaced, I ate, or worse, cut. I hated my mom for dictating me and myself for not being able to change it. I have a bad image of myself after all of that.

Burn Your Fat Pants: Candid Guidance from a Girlfriend

Chapter 4

Fit or Fat — It's a Mindset Thing

I think the key is for women not to set any limits.
—Martina Navratilova

Mindset means that you have a particular way of viewing things in your life. It is grounded by your personal perspective. And that perspective has been shaped by the media, experiential fact, and from the influential people you've come in contact with throughout your lifetime.

Through my own weight-loss journey, and the experience in working with the Mind Body Fit Club girls, I have discovered a distinct difference between eating to lose weight, and eating to be healthy. The mindset between the two perspectives are very different, and also yield extremely opposite results.

First, let's turn our attention to the "diet" mindset or what I like to call the "Fat" mindset, and explore its attributes. I believe diet and Fat, are one in the same. If you are always thinking you need to go on a diet, or you're trying to be good on your diet, then you must think, "I'm fat, and I have more weight to lose." This type of thinking develops a Fat mindset that is filled with harmful deceptions. It's not a nurturing place to be, and definitely not a confidence-forming behavior.

When you go on a diet, it is as if you are planning for a beginning and an end. So if you start your diet on Monday, when does it end? Does it end when you blow it, and you need to get back on your diet? How many times have you said? "I'll diet on Monday!" There is a definitive timeline to the diet mindset. It is a temporary means to a goal that has many downfalls. This is how we become trapped in Yo-Yo dieting.

How often have you set a goal for yourself to lose X amount of weight in X amount of weeks? With the best of intentions, you buy all the good stuff at the grocery store. You start working out extra hard, and you even do it religiously. After all, you have a goal to achieve, right? You may have set that goal because your high school reunion is coming up, and you really want to impress the people you haven't seen for years. Maybe you're getting married, and you have a certain idea in your mind about how you want to look on your wedding day. You are on a mission to achieve weight loss in a measureable amount of time, so you do everything in your power to make that goal reality. You have dangled the carrot (pun intended), and you are focused.

While dieting, think about all the extra time you have put into exercising. You may have made it such a priority that you turned down outings and fun things with friends or family. You say, "Oh no, I can't, I've got to work out today." A couple months later you miraculously reach your goal weight, and feel great about yourself. You temporarily worked hard, focused on eating better, warded off the cravings, and...

Oh, but wait, what happens after that time period?

Let's think about this for a moment. Never once did you consider what will happen after you say, "I do." You just figure that everything will be great because you're skinny, and it will all just take care of itself. Never once did you think beyond the wedding day, and strategize your weight maintenance for the future. You simply put your focus on a segment of time.

Aha! A trap! Sorry to have to say it like this, but you are hallucinating, Sista! Because soon you decide that you're feeling so good about yourself, and you

Have the Courage to Learn How Strong You Are!

Burn Your Fat Pants: Candid Guidance from a Girlfriend

look so great that you can have a Caramel Macchiato again. You can reward yourself! Yippeee! That's how it starts...

But then, sneaking back into your life is the dreaded recourse. A stressful incident happens as life is sure to serve it up when you least expect it, and your stored data of limiting factors begins to creep back into your days.

As time goes by you slowly go back to your old habits, and end up gaining the weight back. You're left disgusted, disappointed, and wishing for your skinny jeans to fit you again.

Whew...it's all so exhausting, isn't it?

If you have not engaged in yo-yo dieting, perhaps you have experienced a Fat Mindset in other ways. Many of my clients have succumbed to their subconscious messages and formed mindsets that they are just going to be overweight—because it's how they are made. Because of the messages they have received by life; feeling out of place because of their weight, being ridiculed and categorized, or the media telling us that we gain five pounds a year as we age. You have made up your mind that this is "who you are."

Our minds are so powerful that we can literally create beliefs and mindsets about ourselves, and it becomes how we live our lives. Everything we do is rooted from that point of view.

When you are dieting, you have a powerless mindset. There are many restrictions you put on yourself while on a diet, wouldn't you agree? You can't have this, and you can't have that. You are weak to temptations, because you've told yourself "No". You have to measure your food, you have to count calories, and you are instilled with the feeling of deprivation. All of which are for the sole purpose of losing weight in a relatively short amount of time. The choices are taken from you, and the feeling of "I have to" sets in.

"I have to go exercise."

"I can't have mayo on my sandwich."

"Hold the bun; I can't have that. Too many carbs."

"No thank you: I can't have it; I'm on a diet."

You are helpless against a much stronger force. You can only stick with it for a short period of time. You feelin' me girl? Are we on the same wavelength?

Think about how much time we spend working out for a particular goal. If all of that working out is not realistic to a lifestyle for you, then it is just not something you can keep up. You will get burned out, and you will quit.

For example: a weight-loss client of mine shared with me that when she was on a program—let's call it...Genny Kraig—she adhered to the diet very closely, and focused on clocking X amount of steps on her pedometer each day. She became so obsessed with increasing those registered numbers that practically all she was doing was walking, walking, and walking just to beat her own daily records. Well, beating records is great, and all in due time but what happened to my client is, she became overwhelmed by the demand of her unrealistic expectations. She couldn't keep up with the high standards she had set for herself. Eventually she stopped walking altogether, and gained back all of the weight she had lost. Now she's back at square one, and joining my program.

Here's the irony: her first inkling once she joined the MBFC program was to dust off her pedometer, and start the whole madness over again. This is a diet cycle, a Fat mindset. Had she focused on a reasonable amount of exercise each day, she'd still be doing it, and she would have maintained her weight easily breaking the vicious cycle of the past.

The Fat mindset woman would not have the desire to hang out with the Fit-minded woman. She may feel uncomfortable and fearful by what seems like the Fit minds overly ambitious energy. Often I have had women say to me, "I'll work out with you once I lose some weight." That is ridiculously backwards, don't ya think? But a Fat mindset thinks of the Fit people as a different breed, they can't help but think that way because they have conditioned themselves to do so.

Have you had a fit friend invite you to go walking or for a jog? And you make up an excuse, or flat out say "No Way" because you are either scared you'll keel over or simply aren't interested at all in jogging because you think "Big girls don't jog." Countless times I have heard new Mind Body Fit Club girls express their feelings of intimidation by going to the gym. They feel like all eyes are on them, "the fat girl on the treadmill".

While running a Half Marathon, I came upon a girl vomiting on the side of the road. When I asked if she's okay, she answered, "Yeah, it's just nerves." I asked her what her anxiety was about, she said, "I just want to finish." As I probed her, and asked more questions, she divulged that she had all the negative messages of her life circling in her head. She thought about how many times she was ridiculed for being fat, and how the overall message from society is that fat girls don't run.

She was on mile five out of thirteen, and she was running. Yet, her mental language was so strong that it made her physically sick, and she doubted her performance. On that day, she was choosing to listen to her old programming.

The negative language we allow ourselves to engage in is really all nonsense that we've made up in our minds. So how do you get out of this trap, and start to shape your mind with purposeful intention? How do we get rid of old thinking, and create new perspectives? I'm about to share it with you, and it will be easier than you might think...

To become a FIT Chick, you have to think and act like one NOW!

We as humans are prone to habitual behavior. We like it; we live by it through repetitive routines and schedules. Having a certain method of how we do things makes us feel safe, and comfortable. Repetition in our lives is predictable, and measurable. Without repetition we are living in the unknown, and that can be scary.

As much as repetition dictates our old habits, repetition is also a key factor in creating new habits. When we do something new, we initially feel uncertain and question our ability. Yet the more we repeatedly practice, the better we get, and soon we feel comfortable with the new habit.

This is a method for developing a new mindset. Repeat a new behavior over and over until it becomes natural to you. It will become unconscious after a period of time, and then your efforts will be relieved to something that just feels normal for you to do. You won't have to consciously focus on it anymore; it becomes just how you do things. This practice only works if the behavior you are working to build is sustainable. In other words, if you cannot maintain the level of time you devote to the new habit, then it is not a habit that will stay with you.

The idea I really want you to take to the bank is this: utilize the methodology that repeated daily, healthful acts will cause a shift in mindset and result in a body you love. And by participating in this repeated behavior, you will strategically align yourself with attracting the support and guidance you need to make the mind-shift concrete. As you seek change, new insight will come to you in the form of fitness enthusiasts and educators;, people that have been successful at losing weight, and supportive programs; all because it is your focused interest, and your awareness is open to learning more. Dieters can easily transition into the nutritionally conscious, and non-movers can transform into fitness enthusiasts.

The Fit mindset creates a feeling of Power

The Fit mindset gives you back your personal power. It offers up a boundless amount of choices. You can make the decision to shift your thinking from I can't, to I choose...

I Am choosing to eat healthier.

I Am choosing to consume foods that give me more energy.

I Am choosing to exercise because I know I'll feel good afterward.

I Am choosing to let go of old cravings because I know they did not serve my highest good.

I Am choosing to understand my emotions better, and make conscious decisions.

I Am living as the woman I want to be.

In the Fit Mindset you are <u>choosing</u> to take a POWERFUL position in your body's health. You hold all the cards. **You become pro-active, mindful, and strategic. This is the mindset of the Fit Chick!**

I'd like to share with you a story about a girl named Pam. (In respect of her privacy, I have changed her given name to a different three-letter name.) She became part of The Mind Body Fit Club because she had a burning desire to lose weight and get in shape. Pam grew up challenged with weight issues; she was raised in an overweight family, and suffered from many physical ailments. She had a plethora of circumstances against her in her battle to get her weight under control.

Over a period of time, between the ages of 19-21 she had five knee surgeries. Her friends and family became accustomed to seeing her on crutches, and she became the girl with the knee injury.

Fast forward a decade or so. When she entered the Mind Body Fit Club, she had a total of eight knee surgeries. She began at Day 1 with hope in her heart that this would be the program that would help her change her life, and finally lose the weight.

Pam excitedly moved through the self-development materials by answering and journaling the given daily questions. She also repetitively listened to the F.I.T. Session CDs, and became a regular on our coaching calls. Through creating a new awareness, Pam began to realize that she had built a mindset around her knee problems. She discovered that all of these years she had used her ailing knees as her excuse to not lose weight. She would often find herself turning down exercise by saying, "No I can't; I have bad knees." One day it dawned on Pam that she had been defining herself through her knee problems. Her bad knees became *who she was*. Everything in her life revolved around her injuries, her surgeries, and what she *couldn't* do.

Pam had not made the connection until it was pointed out to her through our program. Once she gained AWARENESS, Pam was able to bring the unconscious behaviors out into the open. It was like a whole new world opened up in her mind. She was able to shift an old mindset into a brand new Fit Mindset that she had never known before. **An OMG moment!**

Pam had lived her entire life within walking distance to her local YMCA. Never once over the years did she set foot in that gym, or even think of it as a place for her to go. Now that she is enlightened with new self-understanding, she not only joined the Y, but you can find her there more than half the week. Pam has lost over forty pounds, and now considers herself a fitness enthusiast. She is an inspiration to everyone who knows her. She regularly enjoys spinning, swimming and even belly dancing classes.

Perhaps you want to know, does Pam still have knee issues? Yes she does, but she figures they hurt before anyway, even when she did nothing. She says, "I might as well be in shape, and feel good about myself. And if my knees hurt, well, at least they hurt on a thinner, fit body." Pam continues to impress us all with her amazing shift in mindset.

The "Fit Mindset woman" looks for ways to be active in both her free time, and her scheduled time. Moving her body has become an activity she loves.

If you're a woman that dreads exercising, I am asking you to open your mind to the possibilities rather than focus on your self-induced limitations. Put one foot in front of the other, and direct your attention to one a day at a time. See the possibilities for being active as opportunities!

Once exercise becomes a more habitual part of who you are, you'll find that meeting others that exercise is easy, that's when the real fun, and adventure begins! The Mind Body Fit Club girls are exuberant about participating in organized events like 5K, 10K, Half Marathons and Triathlons. They've named our group the Sweaty Betties, with the slogan, ***"If you want to be a skinny Minnie, you have to be a Sweaty Bettie!"*** When we participate in events together, we cheer, holler, and give out lots of "Atta Girls"! And by doing so, it becomes a memorable and very fun experience. Keep in mind, these are women just like you. They haven't always been athletes, but they are learning that they can be.

When you socialize with others that are living a lifestyle of health it is a great influence on you. We've already talked about how the influences you've had in the past are responsible for forming beliefs and behaviors you have now. Perhaps it's time for some new fit friends! These people come in various shapes and sizes, yet they have a commonality. Their unity is, taking care of themselves through awareness of their nutrition, regular exercise, and taking personal responsibility for their health. Dieting is not how they live their life; it's truly about health.

Are you starting to get the mind-shift I am presenting to you? Embracing a Fit perspective now will give you new and desired weight loss results. The process is pain-free, all you have to do is let go of the old you. Sometimes we hold on to our old ways merely because it's what we know. But as Oprah says, "Now that you know, you can't say you don't know." Take the steps forward to welcome change. Losing weight doesn't have to be so darn hard. So why make it that way?

Choose to take on the Fit mindset now, and watch yourself morph into a new woman. Adopt the strategies written here, and repeat them on a daily basis. Remember: make the right choices, and repeat, repeat, repeat. Here is a re-cap:

The Fit Chick Mindset
- Begin to enjoy exercise, and purposely engage in activity that is fun and

sustainable over time.

• Hang out with people who take care of themselves. Watch them closely. If they can do it, so can YOU.

• Have the courage to examine the areas of your life that are not working for you. Identify unconscious habits, and create awareness. Be honest with yourself.

• Divide your bad habits from your identity. You are not your bad habits. Your habits are what you do, not who you are. Who you are is your essence, your talents, and abilities. Start focusing on what you CAN do.

• Set attainable short term goals that can later transition to LIFESTYLE. A fit mindset looks beyond a regimented timeline.

At the end of the MBFC program, it states: **"Welcome to the first day of the rest of your life."** We can print such a claim because I know that if you plug-in, fully participate in the strategies given, and create new habits, you will discover your spirit and make the all important transition into a Fit lifestyle.

In the next chapter, you'll read the story of a girl that displays a revealing amount of courage on her persistent path to overcoming her lifelong weight issues. I ask you to associate your own reasons and beliefs that reveal your untold story. *Continue with courage...*

Welcome to the first day of the rest of your life.

F.I.T. Strategy Exercise

Inner Fit Chick Visualization

To start living fit now, you must re-program your subconscious thoughts to align with the fit-chick you want to become. Here you will use a creative process to help you unconsciously speak directly to your inner mind.

With paper and pencil, rally up your inner artist and draw how you believe you look now. That's right girlfriend, include the bumps, and love-handles. Don't worry about being a da Vinci. Draw yourself from your perspective to the best of your ability.

Next, draw the woman you want to be on the inside of your current parameters. Draw her with the lean curves and strong body that you want.

Have fun with your drawing by tapping into your playful inner child. This is not a time to pass judgment; it is an opportunity to dream.

The Space Between

Take a moment to observe the space between who you are now, and the fit-chick you want to become. The space between is an opportunity to learn, grow and develop. Along the left side of your inner-fit-chick drawing, describe what the space between represents.

- What poor habits created the space between?

- What emotions must be released to unveil the fit-chick inside of you?

- List any feelings of unworthiness, past hurts, pains or experiences that have been weighing you down.

The Fit Chick Profile

On the right side of your drawing, create a profile of the success factors of the fit-chick.

Think as if you are that beautiful fit woman and project the answers from 'her' point of view.

- What does your fit-chick eat for energy?
- What is her schedule like? Does she create time to exercise and plan her meals?
- How does she relax?
- How does she handle stress?
- How do others respond to her?
- What activities does she do for fun?
- How does she feel about herself?

Take a good look at the-fit-chick attributes and apply them to your life now. Have faith and trust in yourself. Rely on your inner-fit-chick as guidance in helping you to make better decisions.

- In a moment of weakness, before you choose to eat the creamy pasta, ask yourself...

"What choice would my inner-fit-chick make? The pasta or the healthy salad with lean protein?

- In a moment of struggle, before you dig into the ice cream to soothe stress, ask yourself...

"How would she choose to re-act?" Would she eat to self soothe, or would she get some exercise?

Adopt the behaviors of your inner-fit-chick now. Don't wait. This process is like a map guiding you to your desire. It engages your immediate thinking and subconscious programming. Even better, it helps you to shift your internal paradigms; believing that you can achieve your ultimate goal.

excuss

free

sadness

happy

frustration

beautiful

anger

smort

emptiness

bold

incompetence

Burn Your Fat Pants: Candid Guidance from a Girlfriend

Chapter 5

See Ya, Eric!

Move to the rhythm of your soul and you'll never miss a beat,
—Vicki Virk

Ah yes, we are going to go there...worthiness. Ouch! Now this emotion runs deep, doesn't it?

Ask yourself, Do I truly feel worthy of having the body I say I want?

On the surface you might sarcastically answer, "Yeah, De'Anna, otherwise I wouldn't be reading your book." But when it comes down to it, do you really feel like you can lose the weight and successfully maintain it?

Although you say you want to lose weight now, you may have doubt that creeps in as you continue your journey. Self limiting beliefs may surface, and be disguised as obstacles in your path. Those obstacles can feel legitimate, and as real as the surface you are sitting on. But they're not real. They are made up of all that we have talked about; the representations of the past mental pictures, people and experiences that your mind has packaged, and molded into your personal belief systems.

I'd like to share with you a story of a girl whom I admire greatly. Her name is June. She is a feisty woman in her mid thirties that became my client by chance. Well, let me rephrase that. I don't believe in accidental, chance meetings, but I do believe in the twist of fate kind. So, we'll safely say that she and I met because it was in our stars.

Before meeting June in person, she spent many sequential days listening to my voice. Let me explain; my husband Troy had met her while out running an errand to her husband's shop. June was there, and he overhead her talking to a friend

The Finish Line is a Gift for Your Soul!

The night before the race, she lay staring at the clock, unable to sleep. The anxiety was so strong, her thoughts filled with "What if I don't make it in time?"

As soon as she heard me stirring in the wee morning hour, she came running into my room, and jumped onto my bed. Nerves had kept her awake the whole night, and she was ready to go get this race started and over with.

When we arrived at 6am to the crowded parking lot, runners were gathering their water bottles, and gear from their cars, and heading to the start line. The three of us sat in the car for a few moments. June's eyes welled with tears as she started to cry. She was feeling overwhelmed by fear as she looked around. She saw, from her point of view, all of these fit looking people getting out of their cars. They were warming up and preparing for the race by jogging through the parking lot. She felt very out of place, and highly intimidated as if she did not have a right to be there. June was downright scared.

We made our way from the parking lot to the start line amongst the six thousand plus runners. As we awaited the gun shot, I turned to June, and wrapped my arms around her. I asked her to close her eyes, and I whispered, "You earned your right to be here. You are a fighter, a warrior, and I believe in you. It does not matter whether you get a medal today, what matters most is that you have chosen to be in the race. You have proven to yourself that you are in this, to win this for you." Our meditational pep talk ended with tears, and a group hug with Jaylene.

You're a fighter, and it's time to let Eric go. He lied to you. He wanted to bring you down 'cause he felt like shit about himself, and he wanted you to feel that way too. Damnit June, you are worthy. It's time to take back your power! You deserve it. You've earned your right to be here."

As we jogged down the race course, our eyes filled with tears. In that moment, our communication created a shift in consciousness for June. The day of total renewal had arrived. Wanting to leave the past behind, she made a concrete decision to unconditionally love herself from that point forward.

Through silent words, there was a feeling in the air that was unexplainable. A kind of soulful magic happened, as if heaviness was lifted from June's spirit. She felt it, and I felt it too. It was a super-natural spiritual instance, a moment that we will both treasure forever.

June began living her life from a new perspective from that day on. Had she not chosen to step out and take on the Triple Crown challenge, she may have not received this gift for her soul.

June later talked about the experience to friends and Mind Body Fit Club Members. She summed up that moment, and the overall day in these words...

"The sky has turned a different shade of blue."

Amaze Yourself with What You Can Do!

Burn Your Fat Pants: Candid Guidance from a Girlfriend

Who or What is your Eric

The true key to losing weight is having the courage to unlock the secrets you have hidden inside. The feelings of unworthiness, self doubt, the ruminating questions of *"Do I deserve to have the body I want?"*

We all have people or experiences of our past that represent Eric. As we've talked about in previous chapters, it could be childhood struggles, a relationship gone wrong, you name it. We all carry the weight of our lives. But you don't have to anymore.

In doing this amazing work that I feel absolutely privileged to be a part of, I have found some people over-eat to protect themselves from the emotional pain they don't want to feel. Others sabotage themselves with food, because inside they don't feel worthy of having the body they want. Some women just don't commit on a deeper level, and give up before they see results.

They mask their negative behaviors with a variety of excuses as to why they can't lose weight. They convince themselves that their reasons are justifiable, all because it's scary to face the truth. And often the truth is...**I don't deserve it.**

I get it, there is a plethora of challenges that you face in your battle. But, I'm going to share with you the real deal. Are you ready? Time and time again, my work has proven that there is really only one simple concept that every woman, no matter what their story, must wrap their brain around in order to have lasting weight loss.

Focus on YOU first, the weight second

YOU must understand what makes you tick (Why do I eat when I'm not hungry? Why did I let myself go? Why don't I make me important in my day? etc.) Once you can understand your Why? Then making exercise part of your lifestyle, and eating for health becomes easy and secondary.

Start making yourself a priority today. Take the time to think about your limiting beliefs. Have the courage to shift them by creating daily actions that prove yourself worthy. In the next chapter, I am excited to share with you relief that could end your sabotaging ways for good. No longer will you experience start again-stop again behaviors. The upcoming chapter will give you a new perspective to this journey.

You Deserve to Have the Body You Love!

I am worthy.

Burn Your Fat Pants: Candid Guidance from a Girlfriend

F.I.T. Strategy Exercise
The Funnel Effect

Below you will take part in a series of questions and answers. The question at the top of the funnel is: What is your Eric? (In other words, what is your emotional weight? Why are you choosing to carry around with you?)

Answer the first question with a one-sentence answer that is specific. Next, restructure the answer into a new question. For example, if you answered, "I am holding on to childhood drama." You would then ask yourself on the next line space, "Why am I holding on to childhood drama?" Continue this question and answer process until you get to a specific answer at the bottom of the funnel. You will have a better understanding of the reason for carrying the burden of emotional weight at the end of this process.

Structure each question with either What, or Why?

Burn Your Fat Pants: Candid Guidance from a Girlfriend

Chapter 6

The Struggle is Where the Growth Is

A stumbling block to the pessimist is a stepping stone to the optimist.
—Eleanor Roosevelt

What is your greatest struggle when it comes to losing weight and getting in shape?

Is it...

Self sabotage?

Your sweet tooth?

Lack of motivation to exercise?

Overeating?

A limiting self belief?

We've talked about how imperative it is that you **get why** you do what you do. Certainly, understanding the deeper meaning to your underlying behaviors is the truth that shall set you free. In fact, in an ideal world, it would be awesome if you could be so painstakingly honest with yourself that you become enlightened on why you struggle with your weight, and then simply just *fix it*. But it's not as easy as *just fixing it*, is it?

More often than not, people find themselves struggling over and again with weight issues, until they just give up. *If you give up, I am telling you, you will miss the long term reward completely.* Because it is during your times of greatest struggle, that you learn the most about yourself.

It is in that struggle, where you can discover your greatest personal growths. Think back to a time that was a very complicated time of your life. Weren't there great lessons to be had from that experience? And of course, you would have never moved into the experience, had you known it would be difficult. But, knowing what you know now, you may even say that you are thankful for the experience, because you learned so much.

For many years, my struggle was keeping the weight off. I would stay dedicated long enough to lose the weight, but a couple of months or so of being at my ideal weight, and I would begin to sabotage myself for a number of reasons. I would have the attitude that I could get away with it, because I was skinnier. But it wasn't true. That was a lie that I told myself so that I could cheat.

The truth was that I had not reconciled my internal feelings of self doubt. I had not come to the point, where I truly believed I could maintain my weight. Even though my exterior looked different, the inside was still hurting and wanting to hold on to old behaviors.

I ate for the wrong reasons, period. I was correct; I couldn't maintain my weight. Not until I got to a place emotionally where I was willing to take a look at my struggle more intimately. I had to face my inner sabotagers, and grow through the experience.

It is impossible to grow from success. You don't develop a skill, or gain confidence from the actual success. All of the developing happens during the practice/training portion of the process. The success comes at the end; once all the work has been done. The real growth happens during the struggle.

Even Last Place Can Be a Winning Position!

It may be true that you've been spending so much of your time focused on how you're going to be successful at losing weight, that you've missed the very components that will get you there: which are, the lessons of the struggle. It's okay if the lessons are hard. They are supposed to be! If it were easy, everyone would have the perfect body. It just doesn't work like that.

When I run a marathon, and come across the finish line with hands in the air, screaming, "Yaaaahoooo!!!" it is certainly a feeling of success. But I would not be able to embrace the success if I had not struggled and fought through the last 26.2 miles of the race.

It is in those quiet moments during the race that my internal struggle is at full force. During my very first Marathon, the Rock'N Roll Marathon in San Diego, it suddenly became quite apparent to me that I had been holding on to stuff from my past. Because I was at mile 22, I knew I was about to accomplish a HUGE GOAL for my life. I had never reached so far, or worked so hard for anything in my life, so the reality of knowing I would finish began to stir up an old stash of memories that I thought I had hidden.

I was running along when I suddenly found myself completely overwhelmed with raw emotion. My eyes pooled up in tears, and I felt my throat tighten. I was moved with feeling. My mind flooded with all the times I had not followed through on a goal, felt regret, or disappointment in myself.

There I was, with people all around me running like horses to the barn. Some runners seemed intensely focused, and others seem to be desperately teetering between failure and success. It was a heightened moment for me as I was silently experiencing my own kind of internal struggle; tears running down my face.

I knew with every cell of my being that I wanted to be successful. Not just in that particular marathon, but in my life in general. In that moment, I decided NOT to carry the burdens of the past any further down the road. I made a pinky-swear-blood-bonding-to-the-end of my days promise to myself. I swore to leave my disappointment in myself at mile 22. It's somewhere between Genesee Avenue and Sea World Drive in San Diego, and I do not plan to ever go back and find it. Leaving it behind was a decision I made in mind. But it felt real, as if I could look back over my shoulder, and actually see a pile of disappointment left on the race course.

My truth had come to the surface during my dire moment of struggle, and it became the catalyst for completing the race and feeling the success of crossing finish line. Because of that experience, I will not disappoint myself again. I will always stand up to the challenge, because I know the struggle will be worth my effort.

You see, in striving to achieve your goal to lose weight and maintain it, you will be faced with obstacles. They will be in the form of self doubt, a food choice, a decision to sleep in or go exercise. You can either, cower at the obstacle and stay where you are, or you can choose to overcome it.

A Setback is an Opportunity for Learning

When we trip up in our healthy lifestyle program, we often refer to it as a *Setback*. I'm sure you've heard yourself say it, "Well I was doing good, until I had a setback."

Let's chat about a hypothetical situation: triggering emotion, which triggers eating....

Julie was doing great on her weight loss plan, when one morning, she had a very stressful start to her day. The kids were not listening as they should. Their lack of timeliness got them all haphazardly out of the house, and late to school. A dude pulled out in front of her on the way to dropping the kids and it sent her stress level through the roof. The kids being late dominoed into Julie being late to work. Her supervisor was not happy about her tardiness and gave her a warning. The day felt like it was summing up to be a crappy one, and it had just started!

Then, right as Julie settled into her desk, along came a coworker-friend with a box of glorious looking cinnamon rolls and scrumptious muffins. She thinks for a second, "No I shouldn't." But she's stressed, and not in her conscious thinking mind. Julie decides to give in to the temptation, and splurge, thinking, "Screw it, my day is already messed up anyway!"

Does this situation resonate with any of your personal experiences? With a strategic eye, you can instantly turn this Setback into valuable insight that will allow success the next time around. If this happens to you, ask yourself What, Why and How...

"What was I feeling?"

"What other factors were involved?"

"Why did I let myself fall for the trap?"

"How can I do better next time?"

The purpose of asking yourself these questions is to understand the real reason for blowing it. Take a moment to think about what is really going on in your head and emotions. Are you tempted to eat the goodies because you're hungry, or for another reason? Is it the imprints of a previous stress behavior?

Implore the Fit mindset and you will be able to take a step back from moments like the one described here. You'll be empowered to think about the key components of your stress and/or underlying emotions before committing to scarfing down a 600-calorie muffin. Ralph Waldo Emerson says, *"Our greatest glory is not in never failing, but in rising up every time we fail."*

In actuality, when you truly do step back, you can use the opportunity to become clear. By learning from your set backs, you are taking a stance in a more powerful position. When you take a step back to analyze, and better understand the pitfalls you are repeatedly experiencing, you will be better equipped to handle the situation more positively the next time around.

There have been many Mind Body Fit Club "Girl Talk" Coaching calls where one of the ladies confesses to splurging during our days apart. She comes to the call stricken with guilt, and finds it hard to move on. I explain to the girls that guilt is a useless emotion when combined with food, and indulging in it is very unproductive. What we can learn from a "cheating" situation is much more empowering than wasting our energy on negative emotions.

You can save yourself from feeling bad, and spiraling into the internal abyss of your downfalls. It's a simple, old school method; **learn from your mistakes.**

I ask you...

How long does it take to eat a piece of chocolate cake? 8 or 10 minutes? Eight to ten minutes of pure pleasure, right? The taste of the cake triggers off your receptors, and you feel good. You indulge and think, *"Yum, this is incredible."*

Now answer this...

How long does fitting into a new, sexy dress last? All evening long? Up to 300 minutes of pure confidence that can last beyond the strike of midnight!

Or, knowing you have reached your goal weight, and are more fit than you have been in years? If you are awake from 6am to 10 pm, that 'Fit' feeling could last up to 16 hours or 960 minutes!

There's no doubt that feeling good far outweighs the short term gratification.

Which is better? 8-10 minutes of pleasure from food, or 960 minutes of confidence, and a heightened self esteem knowing that you followed through to your goal?

To feel that feel good feeling of knowing you are in the best shape of your life, you must be willing to struggle in the moments of challenge.

Next time the goodie box comes by, be strong enough to withstand your feelings of instant gratification.

Beware of the Danger Signs! If you recognize there is a lesson to be learned, and you choose not to learn it, you are deliberately resisting success. The resistance in itself is an opportunity to learn. Again, ask yourself the Why's and How's....

"Why am I resistant to change?"

"How can I start doing better today?"

It is imperative that you use your struggles to win your race. View them as an opportunity to know who you are. There is no such thing as failure if you always transform your challenge into a lesson. Brian Tracy says, "Never consider the possibility of failure; as long as you persist, you will be successful."

Moving Into Action

There is no need to beat yourself up in the future. From here on out, you will be utilizing your inner mind to release weight. All the facets of your character, your mind-body communication, and your personal belief systems will be the strength you need to accomplish your goals. I will teach you a Secret Weapon in the next chapter that will propel you to your goals. This could be life transforming...lets go!

I view a mistake as an opportunity to learn and forgive myself.

Burn Your Fat Pants: Candid Guidance from a Girlfriend

F.I.T. Strategy Exercise

The Struggle is Where the Growth is

Recall two specific experiences where your weight struggle has given you the gift of learning and growing.

Slowly inhale and exhale three deep breaths, whispering the words, "Relax and Recall" with each breath you take.

Ask yourself, What have I learned from my weight struggle?

With pencil and paper in front of you, journal your answer. Ask your inner thoughts to flow from your mind and on to the paper providing you valuable insight.

1...

2...

3...

Burn Your Fat Pants: Candid Guidance from a Girlfriend

Chapter 7

Your BFF

*If you hear a voice within you saying "You are not a painter",
then by all means paint and that voice will be silenced.
—Vincent Van Gogh*

Let's examine the relationships in your life. Are you a good friend to your best girlfriend? Do you listen, give positive feedback, and encourage? Do you tell her she's beautiful when she's feeling bad that her favorite pants don't fit? Do you give her constructive criticism when she asks for it?

You will often go to the ends of the earth for your closest friend. If she needs you, you are there as support. No matter what, you are prepared to celebrate with her, or give her a pep talk if need be.

I am asking you to do the same for yourself. Through this weight-loss journey, learn to be your own best friend. Treat yourself with the same love and kindness that you have shown to others.

Isn't it interesting? When you screw up, you are so quick to judge yourself, and slam yourself for your mistakes. Yet, if it was a friend in that position, you would give them plenty of reasons why they didn't mess up so bad. You would be the voice of optimism, and offer up a biased perspective.

When life serves up a meltdown, don't head for your comfort food. Instead, learn to rally up your best friend spirit to pick up the pieces. Infuse your daily life with the same synergistic quality you receive when you get together with a friend. Utilize a journal to share, express, laugh, or cry. Check in with yourself, just like your best friend would.

When this 'soul searching' approach to shedding weight uncovers fear or sadness inside of you, seek forgiveness, healing and letting go. Embrace your body, and work on it, rather than complain. Be the person you would want to hang out with that is inspiring.

The great business and life philosopher Jim Rohn says, "To be attractive you must become attractive." My interpretation of that quote is, you must work on yourself. People like positive people. When is the last time you enjoyed hanging around a grump? That's no fun, is it? It is unfair to yourself to spend days on end in a slouch mood just because you had a week that felt disastrous.

Resilience is an important part of winning the weight challenge. You can't wait for someone to complain to about your week, or hope that your girlfriend calls so that you can go on about the fact that you are a loser because you ate a hamburger and fries. You have to be the one that plays the part of the best friend, and say to yourself, "You are not a loser, you had a learning experience. What did you learn from falling off the wagon? How did it make you feel? How can you move forward, and when do you start?" Be the quintessential BFF; listen to your heart, connect with your spirit, cheer yourself up and move forward. This method for weight loss is not about one day in your life; it's about the journey.

I had a friend that once told me she was always disappointed with her birthdays. For more than forty years she would anticipate the day, and was continually disappointed that no one would offer to take her to dinner, send a card, or even wish her a Happy Birthday. She decided that she was tired of feeling bad year after year, and it was time for the pity party to be over. So she took matters into her own hands, and made an agreement with herself. Every birthday she calls the flower shop, and orders the most gorgeous bouquet they have, with the delivery note signed to: The Birthday Girl. When the flowers are delivered to her door, she says it puts a smile on her face, and joy in her heart.

As a self-assured woman, do not judge your value based on someone else's opinions or actions. You take matters into your own hands, and create the life you desire. Those that truly love you will support you in your confidence, and uphold you for your strength.

What if I am accustomed to beating myself up, and don't know how to be my own friend?

It has long been recorded by the great leaders of our time that positive self talk must be practiced to create personal success. I had not learned of this process until I was nearly thirty years old. It was while attending hypnotherapy training that I was introduced to the concept of positive self talk, and I quickly became enamored with the methods.

Up until that time, I was accustomed to beating myself up with brutal internal language. My thoughts were often negative, and I consistently talked myself out of potentially positive situations. I can recall many pinnacle moments, where an

Love Yourself as you do Your Best Friend!

05.01.2011 07:25

opportunity came my way, and because I had very little self esteem, I would pass the opportunity by.

When I was seventeen years old, I begged my Mom to send me to John Robert Powers Modeling School. I had hopes that they could teach me the skills I needed to know to launch a modeling career. Even though I dreamt of being in the spotlight, I had no developed confidence or real talent to back it up. My Mom obliged, and modeling school lasted about eight months. We learned makeup application, runway modeling, and how to pose for print work. It was fun, and gave me the feeling that I was on my way to super stardom.

To the external world it seemed that I was progressing nicely, but I had many internal struggles that I was dealing with; the pain of my parents' divorce, school social issues, and my constant battle with weight. I was always on a diet. I believed I had to look a certain way to be accepted.

One day John Robert Powers called me in for an audition. They were auditioning about two hundred girls, searching for the prototypical "California Bikini Girl" for an upcoming commercial magazine advertisement. The job was for a business by the name of 98 degrees, a swimwear company out of Orange County, CA.

After going through the auditions, I got a call-back. They wanted me to come in for round two of the model search. They had me model one of their bikinis, and shoot some photos. Much to my surprise, at the end of the second audition, they informed me I had won the part. I was ecstatic!

While standing there excited about the news that I was their chosen girl, they went on to inform me the details of the upcoming shoot. The woman said, *"Please be at such and such address next Saturday at 7am in Newport Beach, and try to drop 5 or 10 lbs. this week. Okay, great, thank you. See you next Saturday."*

I had a silent conniption in my head. Stunned, I hesitantly smiled and said, "Thank You." I left the studio, and headed for home freaking out! I thought, *"Holy crud, I have to lose five or ten pounds by next week?"*

Weight struggles were already a reoccurring issue for me, and now my body image was being judged in public, and I felt my future was on the line. I felt so much pressure that all I could do is what I had always relied on in troubled times—**EAT!**

I ate my way through the week with bakery items of every kind. As I ate to self soothe, I became more and more stressed that I couldn't stop myself from eating. The feelings of guilt soon set in, but I was debilitated to do anything about it. As I sabotaged myself with food, my internal thoughts were destructive and cruel:

"You're not worthy of being a model anyway. "

"You don't deserve to be there, you're not skinny enough."

Believe You Are Strong!

"You Suck!"

"You're Ugly!"

My inner language wasn't pretty. I do believe the request to lose five or ten pounds in a week was too much to ask of a teenager, or anyone for that matter. It was a very unrealistic demand. Nevertheless, what really fueled my self-sabotaging behavior was the practice of negative self-talk. I backed out of the job, and the 2nd runner up that was more thin and more beautiful than me (or so I thought) completed the shoot.

When I later learned the processes of positive self-talk, many experiences like the one described here came rushing to my mind. I felt sad thinking about all the times I had wasted my energy on feeling unworthy.

One day back in hypnotherapy class, while studying limiting belief behaviors, I said to my instructor, ***"So what you're saying is, be careful what you say, because your mind is always listening."*** My own quote has stuck with me ever since. I continue to say it to myself as a reminder to keep my thoughts focused on what I want, instead of what I don't want.

When those words came to my mind, it was an OMG Moment! ("Oh My Gosh, I can't believe I've been doing that to myself!")

It's so true. Our thoughts are powerful; they are the seeds that compose our internal beliefs about ourselves. If we water, and cultivate our thoughts, they will grow into actions, and sprout into a tangible, physical reality.

John Addison, an accomplished composer and Academy award winner says, "You've got to win in your mind before you win in your life."

We must be scrupulous in the thoughts we choose. Our thoughts, positive or negative, will create a result, guaranteed. Our minds are resourceful, and will always gravitate towards an outcome that proves ourselves right. Just like I did in the seventeen year old modeling job, I believed I was not worthy of the part, and I proved myself right. The outcome gave me a reason to say to myself, "See, I told you. You could never be a model."

Negative thinking is toxic to your goals, and aspirations. If you had a gallon of clear water in a bucket, and you dropped in just one ounce of white paint, your water would become clouded, infiltrating the clarity of the other one hundred twenty seven ounces. Just like the paint, negative, sabotaging thoughts hinder your success, and muddy up your vision of what is really possible for you.

Your Mind is constantly talking to your Body. We know it as Mind-Body Communication

We are going to take the quote I shared with you, "Be careful what you say, because your mind is always listening", and kick it up a notch.

"Be mindful of what you're thinking, because your body is receiving."

You are responsible for the physical shape your body is in. The quote above should drive the point home, big time! Read it again.

Your mind is absolutely creating your physical results. As you learned in Chapter 3, 90% of your power comes from your subconscious mind. Your stored thoughts, feelings and experiences are creating the body you have now.

Everything you say and do is being recorded by all levels of your consciousness. Physical, mental, emotional, spiritual, and even at a cellular level; your mind is archiving your thoughts and actions at all times.

The mind-body-spirit is an intense relationship, intricately connected as one. How is it that you can produce real, physical tears from simply watching a movie that is a rehearsed scene of two people you don't even know? It's because your mind-body-spirit are linked. You are emotionally invested in an image, thought or idea.

It's truly amazing that you can make yourself physically sick from mental worry, literally having to vomit from a life situation that you are struggling with, or break out in hives from stress. Your mind and spirit are powerful, and are truly the control panel for your body.

Have you heard a story where it was said? "His spirit kept him alive." His spirit, meaning his mind, soul, inner strength; kept his physical (tangible, breakable, real) body alive. That is powerful. His mind and spirit (and help from his God) is what kept his heart beating. That is an example of how powerful your inner spirit is to this process.

Your mind and spirit are what you must engage first in order to lose weight. (Heavy sigh...) And to think, you've been so focused on just what you put into your mouth.

Inner Mind

Let's take a look at how your inner mind relates to food. Everything we think is in pictures. If I ask you to think of an apple, it suddenly flashes on the screen of your mind. It's even in vivid details—you can instantly describe the color, the shape, and the texture. If I say, "DON'T THINK OF AN ICE CREAM!" Suddenly an ice cream flashes into your mind. It may be a cone, a cup, chocolate chip or rainbow; your mind creates an image of an ice cream whether I told you to think of an ice cream, or not.

When you are trying to eat only healthy foods, and you have told yourself that you CANNOT have snacks, and CANNOT have desert, all you find yourself thinking about is what you CANNOT have. It has nothing to do with your will power, or your ability to stick with a program. Just like the ice cream, you envisioned the ice cream even though I told you NOT to. It's just a simple fact of how your mind operates.

Make a promise to yourself that you will no longer deprive yourself from certain foods. The real power comes from knowing that all foods are a 'Choice'. You are creating a lifestyle. There is no beginning and end like the old 'Fat Mindset'. You are empowered with a 'Fit Mindset' and it is how you live...making the right food choices that allow you to live in a body you can love.

Let's talk body image. Breaking it down more simply, body (meaning physical) and image (mind, pictures, visualizations) is essentially what and how you "think" about your body. The same association principals apply. If you are consistently thinking about how much you DO NOT like the size of your butt, you will just get more of the same, a big butt.

Negating certain parts of your body is an unhealthy practice. Have you called yourself, *"Fatso!"* while stepping out of the shower? Cursed your stomach while trying to zip up your too-small jeans? That type of thinking stops here. It's impossible to trade your body in for another, so it's high time that you embrace all of you, and begin anew. Because your mind thinks in pictures, and your spirit is vast, imagine how much you could accomplish by recruiting your own innate abilities, and applying them to your physical goals? Soon, you'll learn to say *"I nurture and love my body by eating well and moving more."*

A New Perspective

Think of your body as a ship, and your mind is the captain. You have full authority of what goes on and off your ship. You determine what direction you maneuver. You are responsible for your passengers, the freight you hold, and the documents stored on board. You could choose to relinquish the control, and allow another person to navigate. (Ever been in one of those relationships?) But they could ram your ship into an iceberg and sink you like the "Titanic". Even so, you are still ultimately responsible for the ship going down and the lives of your passengers. Take charge, own your body like you're captaining a ship, and make strong headway.

Begin to practice good listening skills. Listen to what your mind is thinking, and what your mouth is saying. Once you create awareness, you'll be shocked at how often you insult yourself, and contradict your abilities. You cannot feel good about who you are becoming, if your mind is poisonous with self-defeating thoughts. Your Secret Weapon will help you make the important transition.

Your Secret Weapon

I'd like to help influence your thinking by offering you a secret weapon. You are in need of every arsenal you've got to win the battle of the bulge. Why is it a secret weapon? Because positive self talk happens only within you. No one needs to know what you're thinking. It can be implemented any time, any day, anywhere. There is no limit to its effectiveness, and cannot be overused. Your thoughts—your secret weapons, can transform your attitude, and help you strengthen your courage to take a stand, make a good decision or get through a difficult moment. Even if you don't believe your thoughts at first, create your positive outcome anyway. Trust that repetition will begin to create a shift, and you will soon believe.

When you are tempted to succumb to a food craving, you can draw from your secret weapon with a positive self-affirming thought, "I am in control, and focused on long-term gratification."

Next time you're at the grocery store, and you smell the fresh baked bread from the bakery oven, your secret weapon says, "I am dedicated to my lifestyle plan, and love myself for my commitment.

During a social gathering, while others are indulging in a platter of cheesy bread and potato skins, your secret weapon says, "I stick to my plan of hovering at the veggie platter, and I am happy about shedding a pound this week."

Warning: Do not underestimate the power of this tool. Your internal thoughts are robust and mighty! Utilize them to be your springboard towards achieving your goals.

"It's the repetition of affirmations that leads to belief. And once that belief becomes a deep conviction, things begin to happen." —Claude M. Bristol

Focus on keeping your mind clear and cultivating supportive, loving thoughts.

Positive self-talk/affirmations can be easily utilized to help you reach success and for many different weight-loss obstructions.

Here are just a few ideas.

Utilize when…	Affirmation
Looking at your body in the mirror.	I love and embrace me!
Pushing through a strenuous moment while exercising.	I can do it, I am strong!
You feel defeated.	I am resilient and believe in myself.
Feeling tempted to binge.	I am in control and will win.
Your boss is reprimanding you.	I am open to learning.
You've made a poor food choice.	I forgive myself.
Before an interview, a sale, or an important meeting.	I bring value and excellence to all that I do.
Communicating with a loved one.	I love myself, and choose to receive love as well.
Dealing with a difficult client.	I am patient and kind.

Having a challenging day.	I am happy to learn from every situation.
Another driver cuts you off.	I respond with love and kindness.
A co-worker tempts you with the candy bowl.	I am in control of my choices.
The vending machine is calling your name.	I recognize temptation, and value my strength to say no.
Your clothes don't quite fit.	I persevere knowing I shall overcome.
You're fearful.	I have courage.
You're filled with self doubt.	I am capable.

At the end of the chapter you can create affirmations of your own, and integrate them into your daily life.

Hundreds upon thousands of times, my positive self talk has pushed me through to success. I can recall many times running up a hill in the mountains of Lake Arrowhead, and feeling so challenged that I wanted to quit.

If I start to hear myself thinking..."*I feel like I'm going to keel over*", I instantly replace the thought with **"Delete, Delete! I am strong, I am powerful, I got this!"** Because I know the power of my thoughts, I choose to fill my mind with only positive internal language.

When I am feeling weak at the end of a Marathon, I go completely internal. I think to myself... **"You can do this De'Anna, Come On, Dig, You got This!"**

It may even be as simple as a favorite food calling my name from the kitchen. I think... **"Nope, you're not part of my plan. I am more important than eating you."**

Following through in completing written affirmations will be a stepping stone to your weight-loss goals. As you begin to train your mind to think in this manner, you'll be able to create them instantly and apply them anytime you need them... .they are your Secret Weapon.

Say Thank you and Believe It

You now have your mind moving in the direction of your goals; its time to implore your secret weapon in accepting a compliment. I always think it's sad, when women finds it difficult to truly acknowledge a compliment. When you have given your friend a compliment, and she gives you every reason why your compliment is not true, it's disappointing. After all, you gave the compliment, because you meant it. You voiced your thoughts, because you felt it was important to say.

Speak Positively to Your Curves!

It's a true telling sign about how a girl feels on the inside when she can't accept a compliment. Own your beauty, and presence. Resist the temptation to point out your flaws. As you continue your weight-loss transformation hold your shoulders back, carry yourself with confidence, and practice positive self talk. Be gracious when accepting a compliment, and believe it's true. Receive the compliment like a gift for your ever-growing self esteem.

When someone says, "You look great, you've lost weight haven't you?" You will get an eye rolling response, and a fake smile back at you if you go overboard and start boasting all over yourself. But when you're sincere, and say, "Thanks for noticing, I've been working really hard." You are simply being honest and appreciative. When you accept a compliment, remember, your subconscious is recording data. You want your unconscious mind to hear you!

Equipped with your secret weapon, you are now ready to take it to the next level in Chapter 8. Hold on girl, the next chapter is sure to be a wild ride that will challenge you to the core. You may find yourself screaming like you're on a crazy amusement park ride, because I'm going to ask you to start stepping out of your comfort zone. Have no worries, it will be fun, and my strategy promises... you may never be the same girl...you'll be better.

I can do it. I am strong!

Burn Your Fat Pants: Candid Guidance from a Girlfriend

F.I.T. Strategy Exercise
My BFF

Journal a list of affirmations that represent the new seeds you are choosing to plant in your mind. Write ten or even twenty of them for this fruitful exercise.

Tip! A positive affirmation is always written in the form of 'NOW', as if you have it already. For example, the incorrect form is, " I want to feel more worthy." The correct form is "I AM WORTHY."

Notice how empowering the 'I AM' affirmation is compared to the other? Remember, you are feeding your mind; that with repetition will override the old self-defeating

thoughts. Choose to feed yourself encouraging, loving words that will be watered, cultivated and will sprout a tangible result.

1   9

2   10

3   11

4   12

5   13

6   14

7   15

8   16

Burn Your Fat Pants: Candid Guidance from a Girlfriend

Chapter 8

Feel the Fear; Do it Anyway

You gain strength, courage, and confidence by every experience in which you really stop to look fear in the face. — Eleanor Roosevelt

The truth is you've been hanging out with the same habits and behaviors for quite some time. Even though they are not giving you the results you want, you continue to let them dictate your life. Perhaps you are thinking, "Well it's just the way I am."

You and I both know that change can be a wonderful breath of fresh air. We talked about utilizing the tool of repetition in *Chapter 4: Fit or Fat, It's a Mindset Thing*. New repeated actions that are outside of your norm will create habits that will help you lose weight. In order to do that, you must create change. But change doesn't happen in your comfort zone, does it? And that is where you spend most of your time! It's for that very reason, that you must have the courage to abandon your place of comfort so that you can experience the joy and possibilities that are awaiting you.

In order to break out of the habits and beliefs that are holding you back from having the fit body you want, you must be willing to face fear. Step out of the familiar, and into the unknown.

I hear ya, sista… facing your fears may be terrifying! But wait. Before you go on about why you **can't**, let me remind you, there is great reward to be had by accepting this invitation to leap into the unknown. Before you make the decision, let's discuss the behavioral systems of your comfort zone.

Your comfort zone is…

- Familiar

- Routine

- Typical

- Constant

- Programmed

- Expected

It is human nature to create habitual routines, and comfortable spaces; physical, mental, emotional and otherwise. It helps you feel safe and assured. Knowing what to expect provides personal security.

Mental & Emotional Comfort Zones

You can create comfort zones within your mind, pushing down the experiences of the past that you feel would best be forgotten. It seems easier to tuck them away so that you don't have to emotionally feel pain, hurt, disappointment or fear.

Here's a metaphoric perspective...imagine your sadness, pain, resentment, fear, feelings of unworthiness, grief, disappointment, etc. is in the form of a scary purple monster. That monster is an accumulation of a lifetime of experiences, and lives in the closet at the end of the hall (much like filing away any life ugliness into the back of your mind.)

You are scared to open the closet door for fear that you will not be able to ward off the purple monster, and it will consume you. The monster remains contained

Connect with Friends who will help you Succeed!

by simply keeping the closet door shut. So, to deal with life, you go on about your days pretending that everything is just fine, and the monster in the closet is better left hidden, and stashed in the dark.

It can be frightening to open the door and deal with all that stuff face to face. But, what if the purple monster is not so scary? What if, when you open the door and turn on the light, the purple monster is just brooms, mops and a vacuum. You may find that dealing with the issues you've been avoiding, can be a freeing and liberating experience. You just have to have the courage to turn on the light and identify the issues for what they really are. Not one human is perfect. We all have flaws on our armor. Life is about the journey through this human experience.

I had a woman admit on a coaching call one evening, that she realized, for years she had been letting other people control her life. She had been living as the quintessential nice girl so long, that she hardly stood up for herself anymore. She had little personal identity. She just took on the emotional crap of others, and kept burying her resentment. She had used food as her self—soothing mechanism. It wasn't until she started to have courage, looking within for strength, that she uncovered her limiting factor.

Tangible Surroundings

There are other comfort zones. Our homes for example; we have our favorite chair. We sit in the same place at the dining table. We drink our coffee or tea out of the same cup. We sleep in the same position and or place in our beds. We tend to rotate the same foods in our meals, all because it's our programmed experience.

Even our schedules and routines create the safety we seek. We get up at the same time each day, we walk the same route for exercise. When something messes with our schedule, we are totally thrown off, right?

If you are a person that doesn't operate on a schedule, you might feel in total disarray many a times. It is human to be predictable.

Staying comfortable will keep you stagnant, continually receiving more of the same from life. More of the same, doesn't help you lose weight, does it? There has got to be a shift.

I was folding and putting away clothes one day while the television was on, when Drew Barrymore's *E! entertainment* interview about her life, caught my attention. In the interview, she was asked how she chooses acting projects. She divulged that if a script she is reading really scares her, she knows she should take the part. She went on to say that when she wonders how the heck she could ever pull it off, and be believable as the character; she knows that just by doing it she'll grow from the experience. That philosophy has stayed with me, and not only do I think about it often, I encourage my Mind Body Fit Club girls to do the same.

If feeling fear scares you; good! You'll develop personally because of it. By taking action that is a bit frightening, you will be pushed from your comfort zone, causing you to grow. You may have heard the quote, "Courage is not the absence of fear. It is acknowledging the fear but doing it anyway." I love this beautiful concept. And it's fairly simple isn't it? It just requires courage.

There is a moment that you must recognize in this process. I call it... **The GO moment**. It is an acronym for **Growth Opportunity**. When you step from your comfort zone, and feel absolutely terrified, there is a Growth Opportunity. The GO moment is in the gap between making the decision to feel the fear, and experiencing the new event.

Oooooo! A theme is brewing. Living your life outside of your comfort zone will bring you great reward. Yes!

Nine of the Sweaty Betties (Our Mind body Fit Club girls that do fitness events together) signed up for the infamous Warrior Dash in southern California. It was a three-mile dirt course with twelve challenging obstacles including mud pits, vertical walls, and 40-foot rope climbs.

While on a business trip speaking to the U.S. Marine Corps in Japan, I was introduced to the word Bushido. It translates as, 'Way of the Warrior'. I thought it would be fun for us to participate in the Warrior Dash as the Bushido Betties, Way of the Warrior Woman. We tied Japanese warrior headbands around our pony tail heads, with the sign of the red sun, and the symbol for 'Divine Wind'.

Be Unstoppable!

Burn Your Fat Pants: Candid Guidance from a Girlfriend

We wore cute custom T's that displayed our warrior name, and banded together like a sixth-grade dance troop.

At the start line we agreed that our race strategy would be to stay together, help each other through the obstacles and finish as a team. There were some girls faster than others, but it didn't matter, we knew we were there to have each other's backs.

Wendy, one of the Bushido Betties, had been in my MBFC program for a time, and had been working hard to create new habits of walking at work during lunchtime, and making better eating choices. She was really beginning to absorb the spirit of our inspiration in the club.

Her family could not believe she was doing the Warrior Dash with us. She had never done anything like it in her life. This race was way out of Wendy's comfort zone. Prior to the race, Wendy showed her kids the videos and pictures on the Warrior Dash website, and they called her a hero for having the guts to go do it. She wasn't even sure that she really did have the guts, but she was certainly going to try.

On that day, Wendy had her bouts with disbelief during the first mile. Red in the face, and breathing hard, she felt unsure of herself before we hit the first obstacle. As a group we knew Wendy was fighting off self doubt, so we banded together to cheer her on. At the vertical wall, she got to the top and panicked. She felt like she was going to fall, and held on like a cat on a rope. We gave her

Have Courage to Climb Over Your Mental Barriers!

Burn Your Fat Pants: Candid Guidance from a Girlfriend

encouragement, shouted "You got this, Wendy!" and coached her over the wall. As we jogged away from the wall, we looked back to sneak a last glance at its menacing presence. Wendy was stunned that she had conquered it.

Under the barbed wire, and over the forty-foot rope climb, Wendy faced her fears at every obstacle. She was participating in an event that she never even considered would be something she could do. But with the encouragement of like-minded friends and the desire to conquer her weight issues, Wendy flailed herself from her comfort zone and grew a new confidence that she will continue to take with her on her journey. She said the entire week after the race felt surreal. She was still grasping to understand how she could be so courageous. She proved to herself that day that she is worth the effort and CAN DO IT. She said on our coaching call the following week that she now truly believes that she can lose the weight. Warrior Dash provided Wendy with a beacon of light, revealing to her a path through her journey. Had she not felt the fear and did it anyway, Wendy would not have the gift of 'belief in herself'.

Have you been staying the same weight, and or gaining it back due to Fear?

The Evil Twin

The sister of fear is worry. Both go hand in hand synergistically. Had Wendy worried that she would not finish, she may not have even shown up that day. Engaging in worry is using your mind for negative energy. By doing so, you are creating affirmations that are not positive seeds of thought.

Are you worried, and making up potential outcomes before you even get started?

You may be making up reasons that are not valid; composed of....."What Ifs?"

- <u>What if</u> I can't do it?

- I can't run. <u>What if</u> I have a heart attack?

- I don't go to the gym. <u>What if</u> I look like the fat girl on the treadmill?

- <u>What if</u> this program doesn't work for me?

- <u>What if</u> I gain all the weight back?

- I'm afraid to walk by myself. <u>What if</u> I get mugged or there are animals loose?

- I'm too fat to exercise. <u>What if</u> I hurt myself?

Before you proceed with any more What Ifs, Fears or Excuses, allow yourself the freedom to be done with this type of thinking. Decide to abandon the ole' comfort zone, and attract the people, and tools you need to be successful by directing your mind towards your goals.

To Reach from your Comfort Zone, Ask for Guidance

I believe that people come into our lives for a specific purpose. It could be that there is a lesson for us to learn, and that person is there to teach it to us. Some are in our lives for a lifetime, others for brief months, or a few years. These people are Mentors. They don't look a certain way, or wear a uniform for recognition. They come in many forms, and in all walks of life. But they are very useful, and vital to our growth.

Our need for human bond is what enables these soulful connections to create personal growth within us. Knowing that another person believes in you, or sees in you a spark that others don't, is what keeps our hope alive. When another person **gets you**, it allows you to feel validated and significant in the world. I believe having a mentor is a key component to our personal success.

At one point in my career, while in search of the next level of my growth, I knew that a mentor would be necessary for me to continue an upwardly mobile pace. Many of the personal development gurus that I would listen to spoke about the importance of having mentors in your life. They talked about aligning yourself with people you want to be like, and becoming highly selective of your friends, choosing to spend time with those that add value to your life, and make you want to strive to be a better person.

I didn't really have any successful friends. Most of my friends were treading water just like me. And I don't mean to say that my friends were losers. I'm just stating that in my view I knew no one that seemed to have the whole package. Some had money, but were really screwed up in their personal lives. Some were very happy people, but were totally broke. Others were really good at their career, but they could not seem to keep a relationship together.

I wanted the kind of mentor that the gurus had talked about, so I started asking God for a mentor. Or, you could say, I put it out there.

During that time, we had planned a family vacation with my favorite sister-in-law to go to Hawaii. She would bring her two girls, we'd bring our kids, and we'd spend the week soaking up the island vibe.

My sister-in-law had started running a couple of years prior, and by this time was diligently running four or five times a week. She's a beautiful woman my same age with a very outgoing personality, and successful in her own right. She had been through an unsettling divorce, and a very trying time in her life, but had come through it with what I viewed as strength and courage.

I knew my sister-in-law would be bringing her running shoes to Hawaii, and I wanted to keep up with her. After all, she was a woman that I admired. She had qualities that I respected, and those qualities made me want to dig deep and find them within myself. So if she asked me to run with her, then I was prepared to step up to the plate and say, "Yes!"

The day before my plane departed, I went down to my local discount shoe store and purchased a pair of forty dollar running shoes. I packed them in my carry-on bag, and was ready to put them to good use.

There is something very important to this story, that you must know: **I was not**

Be Daring...
You Can Always Do More
Than You Think You Can!

a runner. I had not put on a pair of running shoes since the fifth grade. I was the kind of girl that failed P.E. in high school, because I refused to dress out. I thought polyester was an insult to the fashion industry, so I refused to wear those lame uniforms. I was more into ditching P.E. and smoking cloves behind the bleachers.

Our first morning there, I awakened to the sound of the ocean. I could smell the sweet scent of hibiscus growing outside our condo window, and I couldn't wait to get out into the Hawaiian sun.

Just as I predicted, my sister-in-law soon knocked on my condo door. When I opened the door to her cheerful face (she's a morning person) she said, "You wanna go for a jog?" I was pleased to oblige. I looked to her as a woman of confidence, a girl that had direction in her life. I wanted to be around her because of that, so I was excited to engage in an activity with her.

Each morning we jogged down Alii Drive, a palm tree lined road that hugs the white, sandy beaches of the Kona Coast. We'd run 2.5 miles south to a gorgeous public beach, quickly grab a cool drink of water from the faucet, and continue the jog back the 2.5 miles to our condos. There were moments I didn't think I could continue, and by day three I had a blister or two on my toes, and my calves were aching. I would crawl out of bed walking like Donald Duck with sore muscles. But, I would stretch, drink some fresh mango guava juice, and I was up for the challenge again.

A Mentor Will Make You Want to Reach Farther!

Our families had an awesome vacation together. The day we left the quaint Kona village, we all felt relaxed, rejuvenated and happy about the time we had spent together. But, I got on that Hawaiian flower-clad plane feeling proud of myself. I had run 35 miles that week! Had it not been for my super-hero sister-in-law, I would not have had that experience, nor the gift of accomplishment. I wouldn't have done it on my own.

A mentor can help you to the next level of your life. They may not even know they are mentoring you, but the point is—when someone shows up in your life that challenges you, be ready to say "Yes, I'll take that challenge". I had asked for a Mentor, and not only did she show up, but she did so with a success tool in hand, in the form of running.

Like a relay race, my sister-in-law passed the baton, and enabled me to continue my journey of personal development.

Prove to yourself you want it

You've already read the many running stories infused throughout this book, so now you know how I became a runner. It was because of my sister-in-laws influence. But how does one go from running casually on vacation, to becoming a marathoner? It happens by saying, "Yes" to an opportunity.

Continuing the five mile increments I had run in Hawaii had been a challenge in the hilly terrain of my hometown, but I slowly increased my ability. With continued practice, and training I was able to breakthrough my limitations and run my very first race, a local 10K (6.2 miles). It felt like an incredible accomplishment. So, I said "Yes" to one of our members when she proposed the idea to participate in a Women's Half Marathon.

I am always pushing the ladies in my program to **step out of their comfort zone**. So, when this idea was brought to the weekly coaching call, I knew I needed to take my own advice. During that week I went online to check out the details of the race. Thirteen miles was bigger than I could imagine. I was nervous about signing up.

That little voice inside my head, you know the one; the voice that sometimes says nice things, and other times is mean and sabotaging? That voice kept urging, *"Do the Full Marathon — 26.2 miles."* I thought, *"My Gosh, there is no way! I'm no athlete."*

Well, because I truly believe in what I am preaching, and I refuse to listen to negative self talk, I decided to listen to my intuition and sign up for the full, twenty-six-mile marathon. I can remember my hand shaking as I maneuvered my mouse down the sign up page to click on the Marathon button. I filled in my information, entered my credit card, and clicked Submit. "YIKES!!!!", I thought. I could hardly believe what I had just signed up for. I was terrified! I was definitely outside, WAY OUTSIDE my comfort zone.

Slowly I learned to run longer miles. I subscribed to Runner's World magazine, and signed up for an online training program by renowned running coach, Hal

Higdon. I knew that I needed to learn how one trains to run a marathon. How many miles do I train? How often? What do I eat to fuel my body? What about recovery after runs? I had many questions, and searched for resources to answer them.

I steadily increased my strength and stamina. I found it to be liberating, and fun. There was a time that I could not fathom running past five miles, but I knew that I had my girls counting on me to follow through. I reported in to them on our weekly coaching calls so that they could track my progress, and be inspired to move more too. My motivation was absolutely to prove it could be done. After all, I'm no athlete; just a mother of three with ambition.

Building up to Marathon Day, I signed up for the City of Angels Half Marathon. The race went from Griffith Park to downtown Los Angeles. I secured reservations at a hotel for the night before the race, and arranged for my Mom to accompany me, and watch my kids.

I awoke at 5:30 a.m. with jitters; nervous about the race. Downing a protein/carb bar, and throwing on my running gear, I headed for the bus pickup that shuttles runners to the start line. I was greeted by a major let down. Unfortunately, I missed the shuttle, and arrived fifteen minutes after the last scheduled departure. Certainly this was no one's fault but my own. I had thought I had all the details in order, but I missed this one SUPER important detail! I thought to myself in sarcastic disgust, " Hello De'Anna there was a time schedule??!!!!"

I was forced to make a decision; either turn back and not participate, or figure out a way to get to the start line ten miles away. Just then, two women walked up ranting about how they missed the bus too. They said they were going to catch a taxi, and I asked if I could come along with them. I had no money on me, just my cell phone. I was very pleased when they obliged my friendly request.

The taxi driver took us up, and over a Los Angeles hill and continued six or seven miles until we arrived at the closest point to the start line. He pulled over at the intersection, and it was clear the race was just down the way. Race barriers were setup, and policeman stood along the intersection directing traffic. I jumped out of the taxi thanking the two kind women, and ran towards what I believed to be the start line. As I hurried, I confirmed with the policemen the direction to the start, and he pointed me down the paved, tree lined drive.

Jogging down the road, I expected to see the thousands of runners, the volunteers, and the big start line excitement any minute. But no such luck. I continued my jogging pace down the road thinking the start line had to be just around the corner, when I began to see runners coming toward me going the opposite direction. I thought, *"Uh-Oh, the race has started! And I'm not in it. Run Faster!"*

On that sunny December morning, I ran three miles just to get to the start line. My hard earned months of training lead me to this day to run the 13.1 miles I had trained for. But now I am finding myself mentally challenged with the prospect ahead of me that I would be running a 16.1 mile race.

Feeling a slight sense of defeat, I jogged on with all the courage I could muster. I did not want to be a quitter. I knew that I must re-strategize my thinking, mentally adjust to the idea of running 16.1 miles, and basically, **suck it up**.

When I finally arrived at the start line, everyone but one man was gone. The volunteers had already left for the finish line, the tables and easy-up tents were broken down, and the runners were long gone down the road, and out of sight. The one race official present was breaking down the trussing at the start line. He saw me running over, and I anxiously asked him, "Am I too late?" He answered, "No, just cross the line so that your electronic tag registers that you are in the race." I did just that, and he pulled the electronic cable up right after I passed.

I was literally the **LAST** runner in the race. A few yards past the start line, the race official came running up to inform me that I was the **LAST** runner in the race. "This was not something I needed to be informed about", I thought with sarcasm. It was obvious by the abandoned scene. He told me to not feel pressured, and to just have fun. I thought, "Yeah, okay, no pressure, there's just 6,210 people ahead of me." I had not come to win the race, but heck; nobody wants to be dead last.

After he left me, I felt a few tears stream down my cheek. My tears were that of relief and joy, after all, I had to run just to get to the start line. I had proven to myself that I wanted to be there. I was committing to complete this race no matter what, and that gave me inspiration under my feet.

To enhance my positivity, I decided to count heads. It took me about a mile before I caught up to the last group of runners. Each person that I passed, I would feel good about the fact that I was no longer last. I lost count at one hundred and kept going.

Because I had not trained to run 16.1 miles, the race was a major challenge for me. I started off strong, but by mile ten (which was 13 for me) I wanted to just lie down under a tree. My legs felt like they were no longer part of my body. I was depleted of energy, and unsure of my fate in finishing the race. The only thing I had to keep me going was my MIND.

Have you ever felt so defeated that you just want to crawl under a tree? Or stay in bed? Or not show up to your life?

Although I was physically exhausted, I knew I had to get myself down that road to the finish line. My mental strength is what kept me in the race that day. It was **PURE DETERMINATION**. As the end of the race grew nearer the sidewalks became more populated with onlookers and family members cheering on their favorite runner. Their energy helped me push my body to a victorious finish; unintentionally running 16.1 miles, and a story, and a medal to prove it.

Even though it had not gone as planned, it was a great day. Running had taught me something very powerful about myself, and for that, I would never take back the unexpected course of events. I learned about motivation that comes from within; the kind of self reliance that is only learned through doing something challenging. Although every muscle, ligament and tendon in my body ached, **I received a gift for my soul.**

There were many opportunities during my race day experience that I could have given up. When I missed the bus, I could have gone back to the hotel angry, and blamed my mishap on the race coordinators. When I learned the race had already started, I could have disappointingly quit and turned back. When I arrived at the start line, and realized I was **dead last**, I could have said, "Screw It!" But, instead of creating drama, I took personal responsibility, and created an opportunity for learning so that I could keep my mobility moving in the right direction.

How many times have you given up on yourself?

How long are you going to keep that up?

How much do you want to attain the fit body you're dreaming about? You've got to re-assess your race. Realize the obstacles that have come into your life are not deal breakers. Re-evaluate your plan, and break out of your comfort zone. Stop asking What If and start taking action.

It will take guts on your part. When a neighbor brings you a plate of cookies as a nice gesture, you have a choice, eat the plate of cookies yourself or give them away. When you've had a stressful day, and your first response is to eat, have the strength to know that devouring the cookies is not part of your new mindset plan.

Prove you want it by believing in yourself. Ask, **Am I willing to face my fears to achieve the body I want?**

In the next chapter, you will learn simple and effective mindset strategies that you can apply to eating. I have shared these insights with women across the nation, and it has helped them to lose up to a hundred pounds the natural way! You will learn how to direct your mind toward your goals and begin to love the foods that will help you attain the body you want. Making an eating choice starts in your mind. And that, is precisely where I will help you to make a mind-shift in how and what you eat. You may never look at food the same way!

I feel the fear, but I move forward anyway.

Burn Your Fat Pants: Candid Guidance from a Girlfriend

F.I.T. Strategy Exercise

Feel the Fear; Do It Anyway

After reading this chapter you have now established awareness in recognizing an opportunity to grow. Over the next few days keep your mind open to these opportunities. Come back and describe a 'GO Moment' here.

Burn Your Fat Pants: Candid Guidance from a Girlfriend

Chapter 9

Eat for Energy

If hunger is not the problem, then eating is not the solution.
—Anonymous

Food, glorious food! Just like the song from the play *Oliver*, food is glorious and does taste scrumptious. There is just no way around it. Our taste buds are vibrantly alive, and when food comes in contact with our taste sensors, it triggers off a behavioral response. The taste of food makes us feel good.

Blending emotion with food has become our way of life. We celebrate with food at parties, holidays and special occasions. We cry with food when we are suffering a breakup. We feel less lonely when we have food to curl up with on the couch, or to accompany us while on the computer.

Food is an easy fix, readily accessible to get our hands on, and it delivers maximum reward. That is…until our pants no longer fit. The formula of eat and be happy has some major cracks in it. The fool proof "feel good" formula isn't so fool proof.

It's time to create a new perspective on what food can really do for you. Food is literal energy for our bodies. We cannot survive without nourishment. As our intricate system breaks down the food we ingest, it prepares to send nutrients to many different areas of the body.

The bodies' nourishment process is brilliant, but let's be honest, Sista, you are not just eating to deliver nutrients to your cells, you are often eating because of taste, emotion, habits and personal belief systems.

You may have forgotten food's true purpose, and you are utilizing eating time for your purpose—emotional well being. How often have you chosen your meal selection based on how you feel? Think to yourself for a moment...do you say, "Hmmm...what do I feel like eating?"

What I'd like to accomplish in this chapter is the beginning of a mind shift in regard to what you choose to put in your mouth. I'd like to help you begin to recognize food as ENERGY. My goal is for you to be able to look at several food choices, and absolutely know which is the right choice for fat burning.

Beyond just knowing, my higher purpose is for you to want to make that choice. This is where it is imperative that you engage in mental reconditioning. I'll help you start the process of shifting your mind. I'll provide you with a new perspective, and F.I.T. session exercise tools to help you solidify your new thinking within the subconscious. With your empowered new thinking, you can then begin the process of putting it to action.

Begin to decipher a Trick from a Treat

<u>Homemade hot fudge sundaes don't really satisfy you.</u>

Okay, you might have just said, *"Bull-ogney, De'Anna hot fudge sundaes are to die for!"*

Let me explain further. Think about your favorite food for a moment. (The food that you find yourself drawn to even though you know you should not be eating it.) Now to lose weight, you know you must curb your desire for that food, but perhaps the thought of having to let it go makes you feel reluctant. You may be convinced that you cannot live without it.

I would like to suggest that somewhere along your life that particular food gave you the kind of comfort, or emotional fulfillment that you needed. Perhaps your Mom served it as a treat, and when you eat it, you feel like you're "home". Or, maybe a few chocolates are exactly what you need when feeling stress. Just a few really helps to take the edge off, and provides you with relief.

That food resonates with you, speaks to your emotions, and it makes you feel good. Think back to the time of your life when you started eating that favorite food. Whatever was going on in your life when you began to rely on food to make you feel better was not about hunger, it was about the emotional state that you were experiencing. You have created a Food+Emotion Connection, and it's powerful.

Your emotional connection with food may also be cultural, whereas food is the center of the family. There may be a heavy influence from the region you are from, or traditions that are followed through generations. Heavy sauces, cheeses, pastas, and frying may simply be 'the way' your family has always cooked. These methods have become engrained in your habits, and traditional cooking evokes a feeling of family. It's a treat that you love indulging in and gives you a feeling of security. In other words, comfort food.

That treat you love so much is merely a trick! Your emotions are playing tricks on you through the food that you are sure makes you feel better. It is wearing an "I love you and will always be here for you" costume. It's a disguise. Food is not responsible for your mental state.

There is something really important that I want you to mentally and emotionally grasp. Remind yourself: you are no longer who you were. What emotionally fulfills you now may be very different from what fulfilled you then. There may have been circumstances going on that felt out of your control, so you turned to food to help you cope, or make you feel better.

Are those same circumstances happening now? Most likely the answer is no. Yet, you are still holding on to a habit that is of the person you were in the past. It's time to let this go! Take the costume off the food that has been disguising itself as love, and focus on who you want to be.

If your challenges are not just in the past, and you are experiencing hardships now, turning to food is not the answer. Food is a temporary coping mechanism. You are in the right place to help you get it all in perspective.

In the Mind Body Fit Club weight-loss program, there is a section on emotions and food. It's called *Emotions Pack a Punch*! The materials propose the idea that food is powerful when combined with emotional state. When you eat to satisfy your emotional needs, you will find yourself with a stomach that is never full.

When you say, "Mmmmm that sounds good" know that your connection to your favorite indulgent food is more emotional than you thought. Ask yourself, does the statement, "Mmmmm that sounds good", reach past your taste buds and into your emotions? Does thinking about eating that food make you feel happy and satisfied before you have even eaten it? If so, you are cluing into a **food+emotion connection**. Try it. Close your eyes, and have the courage to ask yourself these questions.

If you are one to engage in this food+emotion connection, know that when you eat a food for reasons other than health and nourishment, the rules suddenly begin to change. If you are not on top of your game, and don't have your emotional well being in check, it is a dangerous and vicious cycle that holds on tight. Empower yourself with understanding your food associations.

Through the MBFC subconscious integration tools, one of our girls learned her food association had been established long ago. She considers nuts to be her ultimate weakness. When she starts eating them, she feels like she just can't stop with a few, it has to be handfuls. She loves them! With careful examination, she discovered her food association was connected to her loving grandparents. She always felt safe and comforted in their home, and recalls them always having a bowl of nuts on the coffee table. Her young mind equated nuts to be love and comfort.

You can move forward without the habits of the past. It may take some time to fully break this connection, but with persistence you will get the job done.

Taking action is key—you must be committed. From this moment forward, you must be fully present while eating your snacks and meals. I am asking you to start eating with your conscious mind, rather than with your emotions, past experiences and feelings.

Get In the Know

Keeping your calories in check is crucial to your success. It doesn't matter what you eat; if you're eating too many calories for your height and weight, you'll gain more weight. The old Calories IN/Calories OUT may be redundant information, but it is also the scientific truth. If we consume more than we burn, we gain. If we burn more than we consume, we lose. Further important, is the quality of each calorie. Even though a cookie, and an apple may have the same amount of calories, it's fairly obvious that the apple is a better choice. We need to employ mindfulness.

People in general buck this simple concept. Why? Because that means we have to regulate ourselves. We have to watch the amount of calories we consume, say no to certain foods, and say yes to others. It's a matter of Self Discipline. But, in general, we don't want to have to discipline ourselves. We want it to be easy.

It seems easier to just take a pill, not feel hungry, and let the pounds melt off. But, a pill won't teach you what you need to know to continue your success. Popular diet centers that provide you with pre-packaged foods are just a grocery store with marked-up pricing. They're products will give you a visual of the right portion sizes, but they won't teach you about the intricate inner workings of your behaviors. They'll just get you hooked on buying their foods. These are not solutions to the problem, merely band-aids. Its temporary.

You must develop personally from the inside out; learn new skills, practice discipline, and live with personal integrity. When you say you want to lose weight, stick with it, do what it takes, learn a new normal. This is why the understanding of your mind and behaviors is so crucial. It is absolutely the starting point to your success, and the key to continuing that success through weight maintenance for a lifetime.

Living by the basic science of calories in/calories out is fundamental. But, in order to truly live by that simple equation it will take more than just monitoring what food goes in your mouth. Your success will be contingent upon your deeper strength, your commitment to living healthy, and your willingness to disconnect from emotional eating.

Don't freak out, there is still room for enjoyment of taste in the scientific equation of calories in/calories out. And, you still get to keep your integrity in tack. Once you take out the emotional aspect, food becomes what it is intended to be.

Now because I am a girl that enjoys ice cream, I do like to indulge in my favorite treat from time to time. But in order to do so, I had to learn to be mindful. I've gone from eating straight from the half gallon container (back when I was a yo-yo dieter), to a cereal bowl (during my path to healing), all the way down to a

3oz. side serving dish that I don't even need to blink twice about in terms of calorie consumption (Life Balance!). And, I don't feel deprived one bit.

I have found a way to 'Have my ice cream, and eat it too.' My secret to developing discipline is utilizing the 'GO Moment' tool. Each time I felt a craving, I would ask myself one of two questions, "Am I really hungry?" and/or "What am I really feeling right now?" I learned that most of the time, I was eating energy-zapping foods to satisfy my emotional needs.

Next time you are digging through the refrigerator, or going through the drive-thru, ask yourself,

"Am I eating for hunger or out of emotion?"

If it is because you are hungry, ask yourself the next question,

Will this food I am choosing give me energy, or take my energy away? In other words, will it make me feel fat or fit?

The food on your plate should be as balanced as your emotional well being. As you begin to create conscious awareness, you'll automatically start eating food for its true intention—For Energy!

The Mind Body Fit Club has a tested and proven Fit meal equation.

Lean Protein + Vegetables = Fat Burning

A one or two egg omelet with chopped vegetables is a perfectly balanced starter to your day. Mango chicken and delicious grilled vegetables is a yummy fat burning lunch. A tablespoon of real almond butter and fresh cut apples makes a mouth watering snack or desert. And for dinner? Fresh broiled fish with an accompaniment of baked sweet potato fries and steamed broccoli. Rounding out the balance includes good oils/fats, fruits and whole grains. But to get lean and fit, eating every two to four hours, and including the MBFC Fit Meal equation when constructing your meals, will get you to your goals at a consistent pace.

Conscious Treats

Indulge in a treat now and again, but do so with conscious and calculated thinking. Doing so will prevent your treat from tricking you into out of control episodes. What you can measure, you can manage. I recommend scheduling your 'treats' on your calendar. For example, Saturday Frozen Yogurt at your favorite shop. Scheduling your treats will help you become more conscious when you eat, and it will keep you out of the Emotion+Food danger zone.

Journal It, baby!

Keeping a food journal is still the best way to manage your food intake (calories). Yes, I know it's old school, but in order to have a caloric deficit and lose pounds, you must first know how many calories you are consuming each day. There may be little snacks throughout your day, or an excessively calorie-dense meal that you're not even counting. You may be thinking your daily diet is not too bad, but do you really know how many calories are in that Caesar salad that you just

My First Artichoke at 55!

consumed? Or the muffin you chose to eat while on the go? Many times it's more than your entire daily intake should be. You absolutely must KNOW that your eating is not sabotaging your success. You want to set yourself up for shedding weight that week!

By food journaling, you can no longer hide behind your poor food choices. Once it's down on paper, in black and white, it becomes the truthful facts. Information is Power! Practicing awareness is going to put you in a power position with your food intake. Remember, we are shifting you from being out of control, to being gloriously IN-CONTROL. You can only do that by getting real with yourself.

In order to begin relinquishing your old unconscious eating cycles, you have to get In the Know. Studies show that women are 74% more successful at losing weight when they take the time to write it down. Think of it as Empowering Yourself!

You've heard the saying, "Failing to plan is a plan to fail." I couldn't agree more. Your food journal is an excellent tool for planning. When I created the MBFC Infojournal, I did so with the idea that you would check in with yourself often by utilizing the different sections.

There is a 'Mind' section that tells you exactly what F.I.T. Session to listen to that day (a relaxation-focus CD). A 'Body' section to record food intake, and exercise-Calories In/Calories Out. And most importantly there are the subconscious integration tools; the "daily soul question" and the 'mindful garden'. Each day the 'Soul Question' is proposed as an opportunity to discover your strengths and weaknesses in regards to food, strategize and connect with your inner self, and understand your weight challenges. It's a form of personal therapy that is healing.

The 'mindful garden' is a method for creating new neurological pathways. The tool is utilized to associate foods with weeds and flowers. The weeds being food choices that are emotional and/or unhealthy choices, the flowers represent positive nutritional choices that provide energy. The overall goal is to have a colorful garden of flowers that represents your many good food choices throughout the day. This process creates subconscious positive associations with food.

I recently had a member that jotted down her daily weight at the top of each Infojournal page. One day she was reviewing her writings, and she discovered that she had been writing down inaccurate information. She was 195 pounds, yet writing down 205. She didn't even realize she was doing this; it was a subconscious habit to be in the two hundred pound range. She had not been under two hundred pounds in over six years. It was an important realization, because she knows that she wants to direct her mind to lose weight, not gain it. Writing it down gave her the insight.

Your journal, whether it be MBFC's or your own, should always be close at hand. If you put it away, and let it collect dust, you won't get the opportunity to review and experience your progress. Measuring your progress is essential to keeping yourself motivated, on track, and shedding light on your unconscious mind.

The Golden Grocery List

With a nutrient packed grocery list in hand, shopping will become a well thought out educational experience. At Christmastime, do you write out a list? You most likely write a list of who you want to buy presents for, what presents you're going to buy, and how much it's going to cost. Without a list, you may find yourself in Toys R Us overwhelmed, confused and spending way more than you had originally planned. Your list keeps you focused, right?

Think of your weekly *Golden Grocery List* the same way. If you were to go to the grocery store and pull random items off the shelves based on what looks good, you would not only spend more, but you would most likely come home with items that are unhealthy, and unfitting to your healthy lifestyle plan.

Do not buy the foods that you know sabotage your efforts. If you're having a weak moment in the market, just walk on by. I've had girls in my Mind Body Fit Club program go as far as having it out with a food right there in the middle of the market. I'm not kidding, they have actually had a one-sided conversation with their favorite chips. Glaring at the bag saying, *"You are not coming home with me. I know what you're trying to do, you're trying to get me to buy you. But no way, I'm not doing it. You're not going to sabotage me."*

Be very aware of sneaky marketing. Many food companies like to splash catchy phrases like "Low Fat", "Low Carb", "Gluten Free", "Sugar Free" on their packaging. Or, they strategically place pictures on the label that we associate with health; like pictures of vegetables, a cow, or a sun. Don't be fooled.

You are a smart, intelligent woman in charge of her health. Would you give up your ability to stay in control, by falling for slick marketing executives advertising? Their job is to make money by selling their food. Your job is to be smart about what you buy, and ultimately what you eat.

Getting in the habit of reading nutritional labels is an important step to making the right choices in your meal planning. When I am shopping at the grocery store, there is not a box, can or package that goes unread, before it gets dumped into my cart. I want to know what is in the food I am consuming, and if it doesn't pass my test, it goes back.

I have two Golden rules:

- No sugar

- No processed fats or fillers

If it has either of these two in the first 5 ingredients, it goes back. Let's clarify the many names of these culprits, so that you recognize them in an ingredient list.

- Sugar = high fructose corn syrup, brown rice syrup, sugar, organic sugar, honey, fructose, agave syrup, maple syrup, sucrose, glucose, dextrose, evaporated cane juice, maltodextrin, galactose, dextrin, beet sugar, raw sugar, brown sugar, white sugar, concentrated fruit juice, syrup, and sorghum

- Fillers = Grains that breakdown as sugar = wheat flour, enriched flour, white flour, cornstarch, tapioca, processed cereals and crackers, cakes, cookies

- Processed fats = hydrogenated vegetable oil, cottonseed oil, lard

If it doesn't state whole grain, it is not really wheat. It only has to be 5% wheat to be qualified as wheat bread. That means, the other 95% is processed white flour that has been stripped of its nutrients and fiber. Anything less than 'whole grain' (white rice, white bread, wheat crackers, cereal, etc.) is just filler. It's like the dog food industry using corn meal as its major ingredient. It's just crappy filler. Your body doesn't need that, and neither do your dogs.

Be sure to choose "Whole" grain for your all important complex carbohydrates, and never eat them without adding a protein to balance your metabolism.

I'll tell you the God's honest truth, it is frustrating when 70% of what I pull off the shelf is not worthy of my consumption. Yet, I do not cave and buy crappy food because it is easier. Thankfully we do have markets that are geared towards healthier products; Whole Foods, Trader Joes, Kowalski's, Jimbo's; find stores in your area that cater to people who care about their health and nutrition. It may cost a bit more, but it's food that is worthy of your hard earned dollar. Your body will love you for it. The highly proclaimed documentary *Food, Inc.* says, "Think of purchasing organic foods as your vote to the government, demanding a better system for mass food production."

Eating for energy is the method that I have used to maintain my shape. I look at foods with a Fit perspective, and I practice my right to choose health. For you, the pay-off will come when you've created a similar discipline in your life. You'll learn what works for you, and what doesn't, what veggies you love, and what breads to buy. All of this learning will lead you to your goal—getting into the best shape of your life!

Live and eat now, how you will live and eat at your desired weight

A good rule of thumb is to eat the amount of calories that a person of your desired weight consumes. For example: If you weigh 200 lbs. and you'd like to shed about seventy pounds, then you should be consuming the amount of calories of a woman that is 130 pounds. Adopt the behaviors of your desired BMR—Basal Metabolic Rate.

Current Weight	Desired Weight
Gender: female	Gender: female
Height: 5'5"	Height: 5'5"
Weight: 200 pounds	Target Weight: 130 pounds
Daily calories: 2200 per day	Target Calories: 1500 per day

Every week the woman in the example will shed approximately 1.4 pounds; a very healthy amount according to nutritionists, dieticians and physicians. The calorie deficit of 4900 calories per week, allows this woman to lose weight in a healthy manner. In a year's time, she will have lost the seventy pounds, and will have done it by learning new behaviors, creating a positive mental attitude and she'll have earned the gift of sustained lifestyle skills.

Calories vs. Exercise

Begin to think in mileage. Statistics show that the average person generally burns one hundred calories per mile walked or run. During our weekly Mind Body Fit Club "Girl Talk" coaching calls, I've heard ladies say things like, *"That 500 calorie cupcake was so not worth having to walk 5 miles to burn it off."*

To start, monitor your calorie consumption, and how many calories you're burning during exercise. This practice will help you create awareness and cause a mindset shift to occur.

Ask yourself, "Is it worth it?"

Is the chicken cheese quesadilla that is 495 calories worth walking or running 4.95 miles just to break even? My guess is that you said, "No." If you choose to repeatedly indulge in a high calorie food knowing that your plan is to exercise it off later, you really don't have a very solid plan.

The idea of creating a daily exercise routine is to:

    A) Create endorphins (endorphins make you feel good)

    B) Get in better shape (increase your fitness level and health)

    C) **Burn up Fat Calories!**

If you're constantly eating as many calories as you are burning than you are simply spinning your wheels. It would be comparable to walking on a treadmill as a way to get to the park. You're not really going anywhere, just staying in place!

Empower yourself with this thought: be proactive by learning good nutrition, and making better choices, then the time you spend moving your body will be quality time. Your walk to the park will actually get you there, and it will all be worth your effort.

Does this mean that your entire life should be consumed with calorie counting? Absolutely not. Creating a fit and healthy lifestyle is about optimally balancing your life in all areas. Once you have successfully created a lifestyle of health, it will be easy and your decision making process will be a natural process.

The Gestation Period

Have you ever said, "The scale doesn't show my hard work as fast as I want it to; it bums me out so much that I just give in and sabotage myself."

Your focus and mindful eating absolutely will show up on the scale. Have a positive expectation of 1-2 pounds per week of weight shed. This should be your goal. Following this healthy guideline will enable you to shed weight easily while learning 'over time' the skills and mindsets necessary for maintaining. As you've learned throughout this book, there is a reason you have been overweight. Don't miss the learning opportunity of a **GO Moment** just because you think you're not progressing fast enough. Think of this process as your gestation period to birthing the New You.

Quit Tripp'n

It is imperative that you keep in mind the science behind your body chemistry. Remember, 3500 calories is the equivalent of one pound of body weight. If you get on the scale one day with no change to your weight, then weigh the next day to find you are three pounds heavier, don't start tripp'n sista! In order for you to have actually gained three pounds of body weight means that you would have had to consume 10,500 calories since the last time you weighed. That is nearly impossible! Those three pounds could be representation of your body holding water weight. Perhaps you consumed a salty food the day before? Or, just drinking your daily consumption of water intake is equivalent to four pounds. Keep the weighing to a minimum for a truthful reading, and don't let a number on the scale determine your attitude for the day. That is of course...unless the number is to your liking. Then by all means, celebrate!

What about late night eating?

It is a farce that eating late at night will cause weight gain. To be specific, it will only cause weight gain if you have already reached your maximum caloric intake for the day. For instance, let's say your target BMR (amount for losing weight) is 1500 calories per day. If you have already reached your quota at dinner time, and you then decide to eat a 300 calorie snack before bedtime, yes, you will be over your calorie burning quota and you'll gain weight (or not lose weight) on the scale that week. The International Association of Sports Sciences suggests food timing of eating every two to four hours is most important in burning fat.

In the next chapter I'm going to continue our theme of keeping it real. We'll be discussing accountability and showing up to your life. You'll have the opportunity of learning how to begin living as the person you know you can be by gathering up all the information and insights you've learned throughout this book, and then holding yourself to a new standard. It's exciting how much progress you've already made, let's continue...

I eat for energy and health.

Burn Your Fat Pants: Candid Guidance from a Girlfriend

F.I.T. Strategy Exercise

Emotions + Food

Play a game of connect the dots. Utilize the left column to write down your 'go to foods' that you eat when feeling emotional (your Supergirl Kryptonite). Then connect the food with the emotion that is most fitting to the right. It is not necessary to fill up the entire left column. Write in as many foods that you can think of that tend to make you stumble. After completing the exercise, download the corresponding F.I.T. Session on MindBodyFitClub.com for a beautiful relaxation session that will allow you to forgive and re-strategize.

- •
- •
- •
- •
- •
- •
- •
- •
- •
- •
- •
- •

- • Fear
- • Loneliness
- • Happy
- • Sadness
- • Resentment
- • Anger
- • Anxiety
- • Frustration
- • Stress
- • Joy
- • Despair
- • Guilt

Burn Your Fat Pants: Candid Guidance from a Girlfriend

Chapter 10
Show Up!

The pain of discipline is far less than the pain of regret. —Sarah Bombell

Reaching your healthy lifestyle and weight goals will require adding character to your weight-shed plan. Amongst the most important character traits are discipline, accountability or personal responsibility, and commitment. The many diets you've been on in the past were focused on holding strong with your willpower and exercising your booty off to reach a goal. Well, no more, Sista! You can't afford to spend another waking moment worrying about your weight and getting caught up in short-term dieting. THIS IS ABOUT YOUR LIFE!

You're going to have to reach farther and dig deeper to come into the light of freedom, so that you can burn your fat pants for good! You say you want to lose weight. Prepare yourself that your character will be tested along this journey. Take a deep breath, and settle in, this might take a year or so. Be assured: anything that is to be sustained requires character. Focus on the big picture of what you want for your life, and trust yourself that this is the right time to raise your standards.

It's never too late. I once met up with an eighty-three year old woman jogging along in a half marathon. I couldn't help but chat with her for a moment; I wanted to know where her drive came from. She said she's run a hundred and fifty marathons, and she doesn't even count the half marathons. A widow of ten years, she spends her time training and traveling around the country participating in events. Her grandkids support her by cheering at the finish lines, and admiring her wall of medals. She had been interviewed by the news media dozens of times. She said that entering an event keeps her in the mindset of wanting to beat her own time.

Unite With Friends
Who Share
a Fit Attitude!

The kind of drive that Grandma Runner has is a derivative of true character. It's within you as well. You may be using your strength of character in another area of your life and haven't directed it toward your health. Or perhaps it's waiting to be unearthed.

Accountability is about following through and doing what you say you're going to do.

As a child, you did your chores, which showed personal responsibility, and you were rewarded. Perhaps you were rewarded with a weekly allowance, or an 'Atta Girl'. Now that you're an adult, you can think of creating healthy habits as the chores that must be completed to reach your weekly goal. Your compensation will be your one or two pounds of weight shed at the end of the week. Some of the girls in my program also give themselves tangible prizes for reaching their goals. At a five pound mark, they buy a new fitness outfit, or a cool heart rate monitor to celebrate.

What if being accountable has been one of your downfalls? You say you're going to walk three times this week, but you just can't seem to keep to your schedule. You say you're NOT going to sabotage yourself, but you do. Now before you get too down on yourself, rest easy by knowing that many of us have stumbled with truly sticking to a healthy diet. Here's some hope: accountability is a learned behavior. Character is not born into you, it is developed.

For many years I had a lack of personal responsibility. I had been relatively unmotivated most of my growing up years. My childhood did not consist of regular chores or responsibilities. In fact, I was not held accountable for much. There was a perceived expectation in my household, but not much follow through in enforcing it. My Mom felt detached. She did a lot of talking, but not a lot of connecting. Not being held accountable had an immense effect on my character. My lack of accountability was a factor that contributed to low self esteem, poor body image, and yo-yoing on the scale. But wait a minute, before you think that I am putting the blame on my Mom, I would like you to know that I now 'own' the responsibility.

At about the age of thirty, I started to put more focus on working on myself. I finally realized that my inability to be accountable greatly affected my weight. I had no problem heaving down three bowls of Lucky Charms while alone in the kitchen late at night. I'm sure you've done it? You know, where you pour in a little more milk with your cereal, and then you have too much milk so you add more cereal. Before you know it, you're stomach is stuffed full and you've consumed eight hundred calories. Eating like that is NOT about hunger. Call it boredom, sadness, stress, whatever emotional label you want to put on it, but it's NOT about hunger.

It funneled down to personal accountability. I couldn't fix the emotional eating, if I wasn't willing to be responsible for it. It took maturity, soul searching and a handful of hypnotherapy sessions to realize, I am responsible for my own mind, and how I choose to use it. Writing this book is my way of shortening the learning curve for you. I figured if I'm extremely frank with you, and give you some insights that you had not thought of before, you would be way ahead of the game.

If a behavior is not aligning with how you desire to live your life, then it is your responsibility to do the work to change it. It can be challenging; that's where your courage will come in handy. I am not saying it will be easy, but I am stating that once you take full accountability, and own your strengths and weaknesses, you will feel an incredible source of personal freedom. This is what "Showing up to your life" means.

Learning to be accountable to yourself with food is about making the right choice when there is no one watching. A girlfriend, or a support group is a must have while on the weight-loss journey. But true accountability, the kind you will own once you've mastered the inside-out approach to weight loss, is a trait you must develop for successful, long-term weight loss and maintenance.

Learn to be okay with putting yourself in check. I often say, "I'm not afraid to call myself out." I encourage you to develop an awareness and honesty within yourself. When you know you've altered from your plan, have the courage to own the mistake. You can't blame it on the circumstances. Like, "Oh I was at a party and everyone was eating cheesecake, so I couldn't help myself." I'll have to call you out on that my friend. If you hear yourself making up an excuse, take personal responsibility. You cannot grow beyond your weakness if you are unwilling to own the stumble.

It's easy to say you are going to do something, and then NOT do it. Or worse, make a promise to yourself, and then NOT follow through to the end result. Perhaps you have thought, "Well, If I haven't said it out loud, no one has to know". You can indulge in the pie after dinner, and no one will know the difference. It's an easy out, right?

Here's the catch: YOUR subconscious is paying attention. Your insides (your hard drive—your unconscious mind and spirit) know better. Your inner computer is keeping track of all the times you didn't follow through. Your subconscious is gathering the information and collectively creating behaviors and systems with that information. Don't think for a minute that you are getting away with not being accountable. It's all being archived.

The habits you have now regarding food, self esteem and follow through were created from old, stored information derived from your past experiences. If you continue to add to that negative collection of data, you are simply adding to the case against you. The let down of not being accountable to yourself will trickle through many areas of your life, and it will especially show up on your body through your weight.

You are the most important person to be accountable to; because when you believe yourself you can live happy knowing you are trustworthy, dependable and show commitment. Having these gifts within your soul allows you to be a better friend and mother, happier spouse, a trusted confidant, respected employer or employee, and most importantly, a person that can MAINTAIN A HEALTHY LIFESTYLE.

To help you in this process, extend your reach. As suggested in "Feeling the Fear", connect with girlfriends and teachers, lecturers and trainers! Create a group of women around you that you can answer to with integrity. Because you have respect for them, it is natural to want to please them, therefore you will follow through, take action, and do what you don't like doing, all because you know you want to maintain your integrity with that person. Meaning, when you want to sleep in, but you know your friend is waiting for you at the park to run, you'll get your butt out of bed. This is the easiest way to support your accountability from the outside. You can find formal groups like the Mind Body Fit Club; you can create your own with your circle of friends, or both.

There are a couple of rules that will be helpful in order to truly setup a great accountability group.

Two rules:

Rule one: The group must be comprised of people you admire and respect.

Rule two: They must be people that you view as successful in the area you want to achieve.

A group I belong to offers valuable mentor services to women in business. When you sign up for a one-on-one session with an expert in their field, or you sign up to attend a workshop, it is required that you write down your credit card information on the sign up form. When you show up on time, and attend the scheduled meeting, your card is not charged for the services. The service you

Burn Your Fat Pants: Candid Guidance from a Girlfriend

receive, often upwards of three hundred dollars a session, is paid for by a funding source, and is offered to you as assistance in helping you to achieve your business goals. Now that's a fantastic opportunity, right? But, if you are late, or do not attend the schedule meeting you signed up for; your card is automatically charged a nominal fee that had been originally stated. This protocol is a phenomenal method for helping women in business to be accountable to their growth process.

Imagine if a friend or mentor laid out ten thousand, one dollar bills on your kitchen counter.

$10,000.00

With the money in front of you, she says, "If you stay on track with eating foods that are healthy for you, work hard to create an awareness about why you've been eating for the wrong reasons, exercise your body regularly, and find three ways to be more kind to yourself, you will get to keep this ten thousand dollars at the end of the month."

Would you be able to follow through? I'm guessing you said, "Yes, I Can Do It!" If you can do it for ten thousand dollars, you can do it without ten thousand dollars. Do it for you!

Creating an accountability system that is successful, is key to the process. Use both external and internal resources to help you create permanent behaviors. At first it may be challenging, but soon you'll find it the way you live. First you'll recognize the 'GO Moments' (Growth Opportunity), then you'll reach the next level; you'll be able to choose 'YOU over food'.

Check out the Full Cookie Moment as an example to the progress you seek.

An Accountability Full Cookie (Circle) Moment

I ate the cookie.

I ate the cookie, felt guilty, but it was so good I didn't care.

I ate the cookie, and knew while I was eating it that I shouldn't be.

As I was eating the cookie, I realized I was "Eating the Cookie"

I ate the cookie, asked myself, "Why am I really eating the cookie?"

I took a bite of the cookie, and said to myself "The cookie is good, but I am BETTER."

I see the cookie. I talk to the cookie. I don't eat the cookie.

I eat a bite of the cookie, share the rest. Love my body, and Myself more than the cookie.

Key Drivers

It is important to begin to understand what motivates you. What lights you up?

We all have very individual motivating factors. What are yours?

If you want to get in the best shape of your life, you're going to have to discover your Key Drivers, and employ them. Dig deep my friend...

What motivates you to get out of bed in the morning?

What turns you on in life?

What keeps you awake at night, and gets you excited?

What experiences have you unexpectedly encountered that resonated with you?

If you don't have the quick answer to those questions, then its time you do some soul searching. With a little mindful ingenuity, and an honest look in the mirror, I bet you could find a way to connect shedding weight with discovering a new passion.

As I shared with you earlier, when I started running, I didn't expect it to be a life-changing experience. I just figured it would be a great way to stay in shape and connect with my super hero sister in-law. Yet it unexpectedly provided me great reward. The discipline of running enabled me to overcome self-limiting beliefs, taught me how to achieve goals, and provided me valuable personal development insight that I could then pass on to you.

It doesn't have to be running. (Although I do encourage you to give it a go. It is the single most natural and innate exercise your body knows, and you can do it anywhere.) Perhaps you can turn a hobby, interest or life struggle into a passion. You could help others by reaching out, and offering a hand up. By stepping out of your comfort zone, and doing an activity that you've never done before, you may find that you get so lit up with excitement that it becomes a driving force in your life. The character you learn can transfer to your weight-loss journey and help you succeed. It will fill you up in a way that food cannot.

You could sign up for a run/walk that raises money for a cause you want to support. The Susan G. Komen Foundation Race for the Cure started with a 5K walk in 1983 involving 800 participants. Because of the determination to make her sister's life count, Nancy Brinker, founder of Susan G. Komen Foundation has spearheaded a global movement involving over a million race participants and reportedly raising over one billion dollars. I would bet that Nancy Brinker had no idea that she was capable of creating such a force when she started. Imagine the spirit-filled emotion she must carry in her heart knowing she's made a difference.

The idea here is to take a potential passion, and build from it. Like building a house made of bricks. You don't start on the second story; you begin at the foundation and place one brick at a time. But you do have to start! Mark Victor Hanson says, "Don't wait until everything is just right. It will never be perfect. There will always be challenges, obstacles and less than perfect conditions. So what. Get started now. With each step you take, you will grow stronger, and stronger, more and more skilled, more and more self confident, and more and more successful."

Even if you are the most unmotivated person in the world, I know that there are things in your life that mean something to you. I am asking you to tap into that meaning, and use it as a catalyst to become more optimistic, love your life, believe in yourself, and shed the weight.

If you feel you need motivation to get you started, know that you cannot wait for someone else to give it to you. You must create it! Don't wait for another person to initiate it; it's not as potent that way.

In one Marathon, I started to feel my energy dip about half-way through. I thought to myself, "Okay De'Anna, you gotta kick it up a notch." But I wasn't quite sure how to do that. I recalled that a good friend with a lot of Marathon experience advised me to derive energy from the cheering onlookers as I passed by them. So my plan was to soak in their yelling, and cheering as I ran by.

At one of the most crowded turns in the course, I noticed that people on the sidelines were just standing there with their homemade signs. They weren't yelling, nor screaming like I needed from them. They were probably saving it up for their family member or friend, but I didn't care what the reason, I needed their energy. So in an effort to spark up some motivation, I decided to take on the responsibility and yell at them! Yes, I know, it's a backwards approach, but I was dragg'n and I needed to do something about it. I screamed, "Come on, give it up for your runners, make some noise!"

As soon as the words screeched from my single voice, I received hundreds of yells back at me. Just thinking about it now as I write, makes the hairs on my neck stand on end. It was an emotionally moving moment. They cheered loudly, smiled wide, and pumped their fists! I learned something that day, and began to use it as my strategy thereafter. It's a tactic that is useful not only for marathons, but for life. The message I received was, "You must be the spark that generates the fire."

Your one small gesture will ricochet tenfold, and you'll receive enough motivation to accomplish anything you can dream up! If you want to shed your extra weight, and never regain it, it's important that you take the lead, and design the life you desire. Your contagious spirit will be a never-ending state of perpetual energy.

Look Inside

This methodology for weight loss involves your mind, your body, and your spirit. I believe you can only lose weight and keep it off when you involve your whole self. Imagine how your journey will be different from this point on?

Every time I enter a race, whether it's with the Sweaty Betties or on my own, I run amongst the thousands of people in attendance thinking, "They showed up to their lives today." We could have all slept in, and had a big unhealthy breakfast. But we didn't, we showed up to enjoy our health.

As you utilize the mindsets and insights provided in this book, you'll become trained and skilled at knowing how to navigate yourself. Before long you will have crossed the threshold from in training to maintaining. The next step will be training others through living by example. You will reach that expert status once you have practiced, and practiced and practiced; creating new behaviors and thinking.

Jaylene, an inspiring Mind Body Fit Club member, has shed 105 pounds. She has achieved such impressive results by following the guidelines I have shared with you in these pages. She was obese for all of her adult life, and is now enjoying a body that can move easily, run up hills, and fit into skinny jeans. She is more than thrilled to fit into a size that she never has before, but what is truly soulful, is her overwhelming feeling of accomplishment.

Facing a lifetime of buried emotions, Jaylene took on a courageous journey to revealing the hidden sadness she stored inside. For many years, she went on about her life raising children, being a good wife, and submerging the abuse she had suffered as a child.

When she joined the program, she had already endured a mid-life breakdown, and was seeking counseling to help her put the pieces of her life back together. Our program resonated with her, like sunlight breaking through the clouds.

Through the MBFC "Daily Soul Question" and "Subconscious Integration" tools, Jaylene discovered that she had allowed people to control her most of her life. She also learned that she had feelings of not being good enough. On a coaching call one evening, she said, "I decided that I'm not going to just eat it anymore." All of us on the call knew that she meant, she could stand up for herself and have a voice.

Burn Your Fat Pants: Candid Guidance from a Girlfriend

Not only was it incredible to hear her own her power, but it was also very revealing. Through her own words..."Not going to eat it anymore"...she unknowingly exposed the root to her obesity struggles. Amazing isn't it? Our minds are so powerful. She had been 'eating it' for years.

Jaylene has blossomed as we've watched her shed her old shell. Her talents and abilities have shown up full force. She's now attracting a new sense of happiness, purpose and more prosperity in her life. People she comes in contact with are inspired by her. The barista at Starbucks, the dressing room attendant, the women jogging next to us in a race; everyone wants what she's got!

As her coach, when I think about her journey, I can attribute her success to one thing. And that is Showing Up. She shows up to her life every day by instilling her character.

She believed herself to be too uncoordinated to run. We even heard her say, "I can't run." But she recognized her self-limiting belief and started practicing discipline. She did learn to run, and is now participating in triathlons and half marathons. She also rides her bike, often exploring longer miles and new territory.

Jaylene has shown up by doing the 'right' things on a daily basis; eating for energy, in the right amount, moving her body, embracing her spirit, loving herself more, and then just simply repeating those behaviors daily.

Repeat...repeat...repeat...each day. One day of success, repeated until it became a week of success. She's lost one pound consistently each week, and celebrates that one pound like it is twenty pounds. One week turned into a month, and a month has turned into a year. She's now 105 pounds leaner, and has completely earned her new body.

Pull together all the elements of this book— Desire. Courage. Action. Re-read the words, participate in the F.I.T. Exercises and download the Subconscious Integration tools. The Mind Body Fit Club girls' success can be yours too. We all have different stories, and varied reasons why we've had a weight struggle, but as sure as the sun will rise again, there is a better way.

Don't ever give up. Thomas Edison said, "Many of life's failures are people who did not realize how close they were to success when they gave up." You hold the power in this very moment. The choices you make right now will have a result in your future. Those decisions; what you eat, how you spend your time, investing in your happiness, will create a tangible result in how you feel one hour from now, one day from now, next week, and next year. Just think about it....Your future is one second from right now. Are you ready to Show Up to your Life?

I believe in YOU.

De'Anna & Jaylene in the same shorts she wore by herself one year ago!

I show up to my life!

Burn Your Fat Pants: Candid Guidance from a Girlfriend

F.I.T. Check List

- *Drink plenty of water (Replace juices and sodas with water; add cucumber, strawberries or lime for a refreshing twist)*
- *Incorporate vegetables at every meal (A Great Carbohydrate Source for Energy)*
- *Lean Proteins—Fish, Chicken, Turkey, Soy, egg or Dairy at every eating opportunity*
- *Replace Grains with Greens, but if you do consume grains, be sure they are 'whole grains'*
- *Vegetable to Fruit Ratio is 4:1, Eat four vegetables for every one fruit you consume*
- *Dairy Products-Nonfat or 1% / Soy products*
- *Good oils—Extra Virgin Olive, Grapeseed oil, Nut Oils, Flax Seed and Avocado*
- *Exercise 5-7 hours per week is optimal. Focus on Intensity as much as quantity.*
- *Consume whole grains only after exercise.*
- *Step out of your comfort zone; Live with Courage*
- *Be your own motivator, look for opportunities to Move your Body More*
- *Know your daily caloric intake goals*
- *Write down your food consumption in a Journal or the MBFC InfojournalTM*
- *Check-in with yourself on an emotional & spiritual level (Daily Soul Question)*
- *Download the complimentary F.I.T. Sessions at www.MindBodyFitClub.com*
- *Practice Positive Self Talk*
- *Practice the Ingredient Rule-No hydrogenated oil or high fructose corn syrup in the first 5 ingredients*
- *The Golden List—Be a smart Shopper and read nutritional labels*
- *Eat consciously and for the right reason. Ask yourself, "Am I hungry?"*

The Mind Body Fit Club : A Weight-Loss Journey with Girlfriends is a program exclusively for women that can be enjoyed from any location. We strive to help women understand the root of their weight challenges while simultaneously teaching improved nutrition, and exercise. Our proven methodology is centered in three foundational principles:

Desire. Courage. Action.

If you have the desire to lose weight, bring your courage to release emotional weight, restructure self beliefs and face self–imposed fears. We'll help you take action by supporting you with guidance, tools and coaching .

Our founder, De'Anna Nunez created Subconscious Integration™ tools designed specifically to penetrate the deeper layers of emotional weight.

F.I.T. Sessions™ • Mindful Garden™ • The Daily Soul Question

Our system for weight loss success is fundamentally based in shifting sub-conscious beliefs, habits and behaviors. We are uniquely different than most

weight loss programs as we help you direct your focus internally, creating the necessary changes at the root cause. The result is a wonderful, external by-product of that process; a leaner, more fit body you can love.

To learn more about the Mind Body Fit Club, visit

MindBodyFitClub.com

If you decide to join us in the Mind Body Fit Club, you'll find this book to be an excellent accompaniment to the MBFC program. The F.I.T. Strategy Exercise at the end of each chapter correspond to our F.I.T. Sessions CDs; De'Anna's relaxing voice will guide you through a peaceful journey that explores the specific topics on a subconscious level, helping you to rid self sabotage and reprogram your inner voice to a positive one.

Special Offer!

Join MBFC and receive $25 off using coupon code: BYFPBOOK